PENGUIN BOOKS
AWAKENING THE ADVOCATE

Matthew S. Friedman is a leading figure in the fight against modern slavery. For over thirty-five years, he has been working to eradicate human trafficking. As CEO and founder of The Mekong Club, he has a business-to-business approach to guide companies in addressing and mitigating the risk of modern slavery in their operations.

His impactful projects and technological tools have earned him well-deserved acclaim. His organization has collaborated with devoted partners and some of the most influential companies in the world in the fight against slavery.

Friedman is a sought-after speaker who has delivered over 2,000 presentations to various audiences, including world leaders and the Vatican. His storytelling style emphasizes inspiration and unlocking potential, earning him the Asia Communicator of the Year Gold Award in 2017. Through interviews with leading media companies such as CNN, BBC, Bloomberg, and Forbes, he has amplified his message on combating slavery globally.

Friedman's has overseen one of the largest anti-trafficking projects at the United Nations Inter-Agency Project on Human Trafficking. He has managed tens of millions of dollars in critical initiatives for organizations such as the U.S. Agency for International Development and the United Nations. His impact spans over forty countries, contributing to the fight against slavery on every continent.

Apart from advocacy, Friedman is an executive producer and adviser for award-winning films. He initiated the global volunteerism campaign 'Be the Hero' on the power of collective action and volunteering across various sectors. Friedman inspires audiences worldwide to take meaningful action in creating a slavery-free world.

Also by Matthew S. Friedman

Where were you?: A Profile of Modern Slavery (2021)

Awakening the Advocate
Memoirs of a Modern Slavery Activist

Matthew S. Friedman

PENGUIN BOOKS
An imprint of Penguin Random House

PENGUIN BOOKS

Penguin Books is an imprint of the Penguin Random House group of companies whose addresses can be found at global.penguinrandomhouse.com

Published by Penguin Random House SEA Pte Ltd
40 Penjuru Lane, #03-12, Block 2
Singapore 609216

First published in Penguin Books by Penguin Random House SEA 2025

Copyright © Matthew S. Friedman 2025

All rights reserved

10 9 8 7 6 5 4 3 2 1

The views and opinions expressed in this book are the author's own and the facts are as reported by him which have been verified to the extent possible, and the publishers are not in any way liable for the same.

Please note that no part of this book may be used or reproduced in any manner for the purpose of training artificial intelligence technologies or systems.

ISBN 9789815204759

Typeset in Garamond by MAP Systems, Bengaluru, India

This book is sold subject to the condition that it shall not, by way of trade or otherwise, be lent, resold, hired out, or otherwise circulated without the publisher's prior consent in any form of bind ing or cover other than that in which it is published and without a similar condition including this condition being imposed on the subsequent purchaser.

Contents

About Me — vii
About Modern Slavery — ix
About This Book — xi

Part One: In Their Own Words

1. Sex Slaves — 3
2. Slave Labour — 27
3. The Traffickers' Tale — 41
4. Perspectives — 45
5. Modern Slavery and Me — 55

Part Two: Awakening

6. Coming of Age: My Earliest Memories — 97
7. Lessons from My Teenage Years — 141
8. Adult Milestones — 163
9. Lessons from the Workplace — 191

Part Three: Epilogue

How Do the Pieces Come Together — 217
Change the World — 219

About Me

My name is Matthew Friedman, and I've been fortunate to work in the field of anti-slavery and human trafficking for my entire thirty-five-year professional career.

I'm the founder and CEO of an organization called The Mekong Club, which focuses on combatting modern slavery and exploitation within the business sector. We employ a business-to-business approach to help companies understand and address human trafficking. Our goal is to empower organizations of all sizes to reduce their vulnerability to modern slavery in their supply chains and networks. Together with our dedicated partners, we've initiated many award-winning, groundbreaking projects and created a range of technological tools aimed at creating a world free from the horrors of modern slavery.

I've had the privilege of delivering more than 2,000 presentations to around 500,000 people, including world leaders and the Vatican. My speaking style, which emphasizes the use of storytelling, aims to inspire and encourage people to unlock their full potential. In 2017, I was honoured to receive the prestigious 'Asia Communicator of the Year Gold Award'.

To raise awareness, I've been interviewed by outlets like CNN, the BBC, Bloomberg, Reuters, the Associated Press, *Forbes*, the *Financial Times*, and *The Economist*, to name a few. This has allowed me to share my perspective on the fight against slavery with a wide audience.

Throughout my career, I've had the opportunity to manage and direct tens of millions of dollars towards impactful projects that have positively affected the lives of countless people. The United States

Agency for International Development (USAID) and the United Nations (UN) have entrusted me with their critical initiatives. These include my oversight of one of the largest anti-trafficking projects in the world at the United Nations Inter-Agency Project on Human Trafficking (UNIAP). I've also been involved in major national projects to combat slave labour and sex trafficking in Nepal, India, Cambodia, Vietnam, China, Myanmar, Laos, Bangladesh, Thailand, and Hong Kong. I have worked on this issue in more than forty countries and on every continent.

In addition to my advocacy efforts, I've authored fourteen books, ranging from non-fiction accounts of my human rights work to action novels and even an exploration of my unique philosophy of time. I'm passionate about supporting film and the arts and have been involved as an executive producer and adviser in award-winning movies, including an Emmy-nominated production and a feature film with Emma Thompson.

I've also initiated a global volunteerism campaign called Be the Hero, accompanied by a book titled *Be the Hero: Be the Change*, released in March 2020. I believe any person, of any age, can bring about significant change through their actions, no matter how big or small. This campaign is a testament to the power of collective action and the impact of volunteering in the corporate sector and within other organizations such as faith-based groups, civil society service providers, universities, and schools.

Represented by international speaker agencies, I've had the privilege of addressing audiences all over the world. My aim is to simplify the complex issue of modern slavery and guide audiences towards a deeper understanding that inspires them to take action.

But my contributions are only a part of a much larger effort in which countless individuals, organizations, and partners have worked tirelessly alongside me. Together, we are committed to creating a world free from the shackles of slavery. I'm truly humbled to be a part of this essential community.

About Modern Slavery

Human trafficking is a serious and disturbing issue that involves the illegal trade of people, often for forced labour or commercial sexual exploitation. It's essentially a modern-day form of slavery that preys on individuals, especially vulnerable ones, through deceit, coercion, or force. While victims can be of any age, gender, or background, making it a pervasive and widespread problem, it disproportionally affects some of the world's most vulnerable populations—specifically women, children, and migrants.

According to the International Labour Organization (ILO) and Walk Free, on any given day in 2021, nearly 50 million people worldwide are victims of this form of modern slavery, with 28 million in forced labour, of which 6.3 million[1] are exploited sexually. More than one in five trafficking victims are children and more than seven in ten are female. Despite these excessive numbers, last year, less than 1 per cent[2] of these victims were helped globally.[3]

Traffickers use various methods to exploit their victims, such as abduction, deception, or manipulation. Once individuals are trapped, they may be forced to work in appalling conditions, subjected to

---

[1] International Labour Organization, *Data and Research on Forced Labour* (International Labour Organization, n.d.), https://www.ilo.org/topics/forced-labour-modern-slavery-and-trafficking-persons/data-and-research-forced-labour

[2] Based on data from U.S. Department of State, 2024 Trafficking in Persons Report (U.S. Department of State, 2024), https://www.state.gov/reports/2024-trafficking-in-persons-report/

[3] Walk Free, Global Slavery Index 2016 (Walk Free, 2023)

physical and emotional abuse, or coerced into engaging in activities against their will.

In the fight against human trafficking, two things are key: raising awareness and campaigning for stronger laws that do more to protect victims and punish perpetrators. Non-governmental organizations (NGOs), governments, and communities around the world work together to rescue victims, provide support, and prosecute those responsible. But the general public also has a crucial role to play by educating themselves and their peers, advocating for stronger laws, and promoting a culture that values and protects human rights.

Much more is needed though, and that is where you, the reader, come in. It is not until we all, as individuals, understand the complexities of this grave and distressing issue that we can truly hope to eradicate it. The first step, to which this book is dedicated, is to awaken ourselves to an uncomfortable truth. That slavery is not an ugly ghost from our past; it is not dead but lives on—albeit in a different, more modern form. And it remains among us, hiding often in plain sight.

About This Book

This book is a collection of short stories, testimonials, and anecdotes aimed at helping readers understand the problem of human trafficking on both intellectual and emotional levels. It is also meant to provide an insight into my journey as an international counter-trafficking activist.

It is divided into three parts: **Part One** focuses on the experiences of all those whose lives are touched by human trafficking—the victims, the perpetrators, those working tirelessly to combat this scourge, and all individuals who intersect with it in some way or another. Much of this part involves first-hand accounts, and for good reason. I strongly believe genuine expertise on human trafficking resides not in individuals like me, but within those who have lived through it. These people are best-placed to tell their own stories. Testimonials such as these were a driving force in my decision to take a stand. My hope is that by sharing these stories, I can awaken others to the profound suffering that permeates our world. It is my sincere wish that, upon absorbing these accounts, readers will see that they too can make a difference and join me in the fight.

Part Two looks at my personal journey towards activism, by tracing my life from childhood to adulthood. This is done through the presentation of a vast collection of short stories that reflect events and circumstances in my life that moulded the person I am today. I think of it as a mosaic of experiences that formed my identity and values. It is meant to answer the question: how did a shy and awkward boy from a small New England town come to be an international expert in combating human trafficking?

Part Three, the Epilogue, is my attempt to interpret all these experiences to answer the questions: what does it all mean and what can we all do about it?

Part One

In Their Own Words

1

Sex Slaves

'I was only fourteen years old when I was sold to the brothel. I was so young; I didn't know anything. I was innocent then. My parents were tricked by a neighbour into thinking I'd be working at a restaurant as a waitress in the city. I wanted to go. I wanted to help my family. I was willing to work. But this is not what followed. After walking through the jungle and crossing the border on a night boat, a van took me to a bad place—a place where girls like me were sold like animals to the owner. When they told me what I was supposed to do with men, I said no, never. I fought back. That didn't stop them. They raped me and tortured me for days until I had nothing left to give. I no longer had control of my life or my body. I belonged to them. Every night I was with up to twenty different men. For years, this was my life. Now at eighteen, my body is frail from the illnesses.'

The account above—told to me by an eighteen-year-old sex trafficking survivor in 1991 in Nepal—was one of my first encounters with human trafficking. In my role as a public health officer with USAID, I had been conducting interviews with women and girls afflicted by HIV/AIDS. Upon hearing their stories, our team was shocked. These accounts were not just health-related; they brought to light pervasive human rights violations. Yet, outside our interviews, this issue was shrouded in silence—no one was discussing it. Why? Largely because awareness was lacking.

Before the onslaught of the HIV/AIDS epidemic, few people, including public health professionals, government officials, NGO representatives, or anyone else, engaged with women involved in prostitution. Society often viewed these women as morally compromised, criminal, or undesirable individuals. Unbeknownst to many, such attitudes enabled the inception of the human trafficking movement.

As we delved deeper into our work, we began accumulating a wealth of testimonials that illuminated a dark reality of deception, physical and sexual abuse, and blatant violations of basic human rights.

Below is a compilation of accounts by women who have been trafficked into sex slavery. It stands as a testament to the insidious nature of this crime and the myriad ways in which it unfolds.

A Mother's Sacrifice

My name is Sushma, and I was thirteen years old when I arrived at the brothel in Mumbai. I was so young then.

When my father told me I was going to India from Nepal to work, I didn't know what to expect. No one told me anything. On that first night, I was so horrified. I fought the man who started touching me. He held me down. It was over quickly, but the shock has always stayed with me.

At first, I hated every moment of my time there. I thought of killing myself, but something stopped me. I always knew my life would count for something. I didn't understand this until later.

I was seventeen when I had my third pregnancy. While the first two were ended, this time they allowed me to keep the child. I never knew who the father was. How could I?

When the baby was born, I felt love for the first time. It was a boy. My little boy. My son.

It was never easy to have a child in a brothel. It was a terrible place, but I managed.

Then something happened. When he was four years old, one of the men tried to take my son into a room. He was a very bad man, one of those men you don't want children to be around. It was then that I decided I had to send my son away.

I went to the madam and told her I would work extra hard if my son could be sent to a boarding school. Since I had been there for nearly eight years, she agreed. While I seldom saw my son, I thought about him every waking moment. He was my life.

Twice a year, I would leave the brothel to go and visit the school. When I was there, I'd watch him from a distance. I was ashamed of what I did. I didn't want him to remember his time in the brothel. I didn't want him to remember me.

Over time, he forgot everything. Each year, he got stronger and more handsome. I could see he was popular with the others. He turned out to be a nice boy. He filled my heart with so much love.

The only person who knew my story was the principal. She understood why I didn't go and see him. She was a compassionate woman who didn't have any children of her own. In some ways, she adopted my son. I was forever grateful.

I am sick now. I don't have much time left. I promised myself I'd make it to his graduation. It took all my strength and determination to do so, but I made it. I sat in the back and watched him go on stage.

After the ceremony was over, I went up to him. He was talking with his friends. From behind, I touched his robe. He didn't see me do this. It may not seem like much to you, but it meant everything to me.

Now that this is done, I can leave. I know what my life was for. It was to bring my son into this world, and for that, I am happy. I can let go now.'

I met Sushma at a hospice near Mumbai, where her heartbreaking story unfolded. At just thirty-three years old, she was grappling with the devastating effects of HIV/AIDS. She was dying. During my visit to an NGO that supports survivors of trafficking, I was moved by her tale, one that epitomized absolute sacrifice and acceptance. Her resilience and unwavering love struck me to the core.

Through Sushma's ordeal, I learned that even amid the most abhorrent hardships, exploitation, and dehumanizing circumstances, genuine love and selfless service can triumph. This courageous mother's strength and boundless affection defied all limits.

Father Sold My Sister, Then Me

My father was the one who trafficked me. He drank every day. He never worked. He sold my sister first to a brothel Mumbai, then me. He needed money.

I always knew I'd go to India. My mother spent thirteen years there at a brothel. Her parents did the same to her. In our village, many girls went there. You can tell which ones by the shiny tin roofs on their homes.

When my mother returned from India, my father married her. Back then, before the disease, girls from Mumbai were taken back. The village men wanted to be with them. They came back pretty and with money.

It is different now. When girls come back, they are shunned. That is what happened to me. No one wants me. Families try to hide it, but everyone knows.

My mother tried to convince me to run away before I left my village in Nepal for India. I couldn't stop her from crying. She said that what I will be doing is horrible. She said it was something that no woman should do.

I told her that I didn't care. One of my friends explained what would happen there. I didn't really understand what she meant. I just wanted to see my sister again, I wanted to go.

My father didn't say goodbye to me. He wouldn't look at me. That made me sad. My younger sister and brother gave me so many hugs.

The trip to India was exciting for me. I had never seen so many people. I went on a train. It was hot and long, but I was able to see so many new things.

When we arrived at the brothel, I started the next day. I was told what I would do, but it was so different than I thought. I hated being with men. They were rough and smelly and sometimes cruel. I now understood what my mother was trying to warn me about. I wish I had listened to her.

I stayed for four years. I did what I was told. I wanted to go home, but I couldn't. It was my obligation to my family, to my father.

I looked for my sister, but I never found her. There were so many girls in the brothels.

When I got sick, they gave me medicine. It worked at first, but then stopped. I lost a lot of weight.

A woman came and told me that I had the disease. She said I should go back to Nepal. I don't know why they helped me. I got back to Nepal and came here to Kathmandu to this shelter.

I contacted my mother. She said I shouldn't come home. She said people wouldn't like it. So, I will stay here. I don't know what will happen to me. I keep losing weight.'

During the time I lived in Kathmandu, Nepal, I had the opportunity to interview this woman who had been trafficked from the hill district of Nuwakot. She was just sixteen years old when I met her, and like so many others, her story deeply touched my heart. Sadly, before my departure from Nepal, she was transferred to a hospice due to her deteriorating health caused by HIV/AIDS.

My time in Nepal gave me valuable insights into certain hill communities that had a long-standing tradition of sending young girls to Mumbai. This practice was once considered an acceptable means for girls to support their families. However, with the emergence of the HIV/AIDS epidemic, this trend underwent a big change.

The tragic fate of this young woman highlights the devastating consequences of trafficking, particularly in relation to the spread of HIV/AIDS. Her story serves as a poignant reminder of the urgent need to address this complex issue and to work towards protecting other vulnerable individuals from such extreme exploitation.

Uncle Sold Me into Hell

'It was my uncle who trafficked me. He owed a great deal of money for gambling debts. Since he drank all day and never worked, he couldn't pay them back. His solution? He sold me to a local gangster. Uncle sent me on an errand that took me down a village path. On the way, three boys from the village, boys whom I knew, grabbed me, drugged me, and took me down to India. I heard them say it was Uncle who made this happen.

I was forced to work in the brothel for four years. I suffered unimaginable things. Things I can't even bring myself to describe. I was in hell the entire time. Every day, I thought about my uncle and what he did to me.

One day, the police raided the brothel. There was a group of nice women who helped us. They took us to a shelter, gave us food, healthcare, and more. I didn't trust them at first. How could I? Everyone seemed to be against me for so long. I didn't trust anyone. But then, I changed.

After several months, I was taken back to Nepal. There were two others with us. They took me right to my village home. They sat down with my father and mother and explained what happened. When my father heard that his brother was the one who trafficked me, he became enraged. He ran out of our home to find him. We all tried to stop him. I remembered my father's extreme temper.

My father found my uncle at a local village bar. He was drunk. My father started to beat him. He accused him of selling me. My uncle denied it, saying that I was the one who ran off. I was the one who abandoned the family. But it wasn't true. Why would I leave my family?

The local people grabbed my father to stop him from killing his brother. It took six men to hold him down. He was taken away to jail. He looked like he was possessed by a demon god.

My uncle realized that he was in trouble. He went off to the gangster whom he sold me to and asked for money. I'm told he said, 'It wouldn't be good if anyone found out that you and I were in on this together.'

The mob boss gave him some money. He said some of his goondas would drive him to a local city. The next day, my uncle's body was found on the bottom of a cliff. Everyone knew what happened.

I never said anything about the three boys who grabbed me. I saw them now and then. I was afraid my father would go after them.

We never talk about what happened to me. I stay at home and never go out. The villagers all talk. Our family is shunned. I didn't do anything wrong, but it doesn't matter. Villagers can be so cruel.

I often wonder what my life would have been like if this didn't happen to me. I would have married, had children, farmed the land, and enjoyed the holidays. This was all taken away from me. But at least I have my family now. They never gave up on me. They never turned their backs.'

This poignant account was shared with me during my research for the book *Captive Daughters* in Nepal. Among the countless tales of rejection and abandonment endured by victims of human trafficking, this one stood out for its inspiring depiction of a protective and loving family unit surrounding the young girl. Witnessing their unwavering devotion to one another left a mark upon my soul. It was an awe-inspiring testament to the power of familial love, capable of providing solace and healing amidst the ruins of a broken life.

These experiences should shatter the illusion that traffickers are strangers, foreigners from distant lands. In truth, many come from within the victim's own community, sometimes even within their own families. It is a painful lesson that this dark reality exists.

However, cases such as these, where the remarkable resilience of the survivors is coupled with the unconditional support and love offered by their families, demonstrate that even in the aftermath of such immense trauma, healing is possible.

Family is the cornerstone upon which shattered lives can be rebuilt, allowing the light of hope to penetrate the darkest of shadows.

Everything Is a Lie

There were three of us from our village who went to that brothel. We were all sixteen. We all thought we were going to be working in a big house. They said I'd take care of the kids. I was happy. They said the house was like the ones in the Bollywood movies. That didn't happen.

We pulled up in front of a place that had many girls. I had never heard of a brothel. I didn't know what that place was. The girls stared at us when we walked in. They knew what was about to happen to me. I didn't know.

A few hours after arriving, the first man came. I didn't know anything. He climbed on me and did things. I tried to fight, but he was too strong. He hit me and told me to stop, or I'd get hurt. I finally listened.

That first day, this happened to me many times. The men kept coming. They kept telling the customers I was a new girl.

That was the worst day of my life. I still have nightmares.

After that, I was with men every day. We never had a day off. They just kept coming.

Everything they said was a lie. They said I could leave in a few months, but that never happened. They said I could go home, but that never happened. Everything they said was a lie.

Some of the girls fought the madam. Not me, I was too scared. You couldn't say no to them. If you did, you'd be punished. What could I do? I belonged to them.

> *The day the brothel raid took place, I was so confused. Men with guns ran in and took us all outside and lined us up. We had been told that the police were monsters. They said they'd beat us and hurt us. I thought I'd die that day.*
>
> *But they didn't do those things. They took us to a home for girls like us. When we got there, some women came and said we had been rescued. They said we'd stay at this place for a while and then go home.*
>
> *I didn't believe them. Everyone lied to me over and over. Nobody cared about me. Why would these people help me? Why would they help anyone? I was just waiting for something bad to happen. Everything bad always happened.*
>
> *But it didn't. They said they'd take care of us and protect us, and they did. It took me a long time to trust them. I didn't think it could be real. I felt I had done something in a past life to bring this on myself.*
>
> *They told me it wasn't my fault. They told me that I was a victim. They told me that I could go back to Nepal.*
>
> *I want to go home. I don't know what I will say to my parents. I did such shameful things. Will they take me back? I don't know.'*

I encountered this remarkable woman during a visit to a shelter in Kolkata. She had endured the brothel for over three years. She had been under the care of an NGO for four weeks and told me that talking about her ordeal was part of the therapy.

Her account was a powerful reminder that the world of human trafficking is based on deception, its entire eco system designed to ensnare and mislead vulnerable people. So deep into its abyss had this woman fallen that even long after she escaped, she remained unable to trust those around her. The trauma she had experienced had left too deep a mark.

Exploitation has pervasive and lasting effects. For this woman, her body had been freed but her mind was still in chains.

The Terrible Myths that Fuel Child Sex Abuse

Few things are as abhorrent as the forced prostitution of children. During my public health work within South Asian red-light districts, my team and I were confronted with a horrifying reality. Certain brothels were offering very young girls—some younger than ten years old—to their 'clients'. These innocent souls were hidden away, living on upper floors in rooms fortified by reinforced doors. The mere knowledge of such despicable practices left me sickened to the core.

To my dismay, it became evident that the 'clients' who abused these young children were not only those men who fit what you might call the usual profile of a paedophile. Rather, a whole range of men were seeking out these children, driven by their belief in three prevailing—but completely untrue and heinous—myths.

Firstly, some believed—completely erroneously—that engaging in sexual activities with young girls could cure diseases like gonorrhoea or syphilis.

Secondly, there existed a misguided belief that having sex with a young child lowered the risk of contracting diseases like AIDS. Quite the opposite was true, as these girls, due to their underdeveloped bodies, faced significantly heightened risks of infection. This misconception led to tragic consequences for the children they exploited.

Thirdly, some men harboured the delusion that engaging in such acts would rejuvenate their own virility, as if the youth of these girls could be transferred to them. This fallacy speaks to the twisted mindset of those who engage in such abominable acts.

Driven by these perverse ideas and the exorbitant prices they could command, brothels highly valued child sex slaves. Most highly prized were girls under the age of twelve who were still in good health.

Shockingly, the going rate for sexual encounters with a 'child virgin' sometimes amounted to more than half of the total price paid for the child. I once heard that up to US$3,000 was paid for a single session.

One particular brothel even boasted of attracting wealthy Middle Eastern businessmen who were willing to pay handsomely for sex with a child. Some businessmen would even fly in for an entire weekend if a new child was procured.

To guard against unwanted attention from the authorities, the brothels kept these girls in isolation for most of the time and they would seldom encounter others. If apprehended and charged by authorities, the brothel owners faced severe penalties, including hefty fines and up to twenty years of imprisonment. However, despite the severity of these punishments, arrests were alarmingly rare. Instead, the police often turned a blind eye in exchange for exorbitant bribes.

I never personally witnessed the very young children (those under nine years old) who had been forced into prostitution. Most brothel owners took great care to conceal them from strangers or law enforcement. Yet, on a few occasions, I caught glimpses of a child's toy, like a teddy bear, in a brothel room. The stark contrast between a child at play one moment and being forced into a horrifying act of exploitation a few minutes later is a trauma that is etched deeply within me.

Child trafficking for sexual exploitation is a grim reality—one of the most morally repugnant acts there is. Understanding it is key to preventing it, and to bringing those responsible to justice.

My Guardian Angel, and I Never Knew Her Name

I was so young when I arrived at the brothel. That first day, five men used me. The more I fought, the more they hurt me. I passed out. That first night I was placed in a small room. The next day it was the same. I fought again. To punish me, the madam told the goondas (security guards) to lock me up for four days without food or water. This was a way to break us. A person will do anything if they have enough thirst or hunger.

On the second day, there was a knock on the door. It opened and a tray of food was hastily shoved inside with some water. The door was quickly shut. An hour later, the door opened again, and a hand reached inside. It was an older woman's hand. She had a birthmark on her arm. I handed her the tray. She said nothing.

For two days, the same thing happened. That food was the only thing that kept me alive. It was a kindness that I never forgot.

Like all the other girls, I eventually stopped fighting and went with the men. I had no choice. None of us ever did.

After a few weeks, I noticed that the woman who served our meals had the same birthmark I had seen during those first few days. When I started to say something to her, she waved her hand back and forth to stop me. She wanted me to keep this secret.

That night, I asked one of the other girls about the woman, who we all called Deedee ('big sister'). I learned that she had been trafficked from Northern India. She arrived at a time when the big disease (HIV/AIDS) hadn't yet come. After twenty-five years with men, only a few men wanted her. She was taking up space. With no place to go, she took on the cleaning and cooking responsibilities to have a place to stay.

Deedee became our guardian angel—she acted as our mom, auntie, big sister, and friend. When I rebelled and was locked away, Deedee would sit beside the door and sing Bollywood songs to me. She would talk about the mountains, the villages, and of simple times. Whenever one of us needed a smile, a hug, a favour, she was there. She would take great risks to offer this kindness.

Her favourite thing to do was to talk about male movie stars—how handsome they were, how much she loved them. Her favourite? Shammi Kapoor. She would jokingly say she was Shammi's long-lost wife. At times when things were slow, she made us all laugh when she mimicked the movie stars in the tabloid magazines.

One day, Deedee died. She was found sitting on her bed with one of her magazines in hand. The news devastated us all. None of us could stop crying. It was as if our beloved mother had passed. When we heard that her body was being taken away to be cremated, we all went to the madam and said we were going with it. She said no, but we weren't taking no for an answer.

That day, the madam, the goondas, and all of us girls stood there crying. She had been the bridge between us all and now she was gone. It was one of the worst days of my life. As I stood there, I realized I never even knew Deedee's name. I'm not sure any of us ever knew it.

After fourteen years, I stopped seeing men. I took on the role of cooking and cleaning. I took Deedee's place. Now I do all I can to return her kindness.'

I conducted this interview at a Chennai-based brothel, where I had the opportunity to observe an HIV/AIDS programme conducted by a local NGO. The woman who shared her story spoke in broken English, which she had taught herself. She said she learned it from watching English movies and TV shows that were available in the marketplace.

I'm No More Than a Piece of Flesh to Be Bought and Sold

'I spent two years in that massage parlour. I hated every moment. I won't even tell you the things they made me do. I feel so humiliated, so worthless. All they cared about was pimping my body out for money. I wasn't human to them. I had to do whatever the johns wanted. It was disgusting and obscene.

None of them knew my name. None of them knew I came from Kansas City. That I had two sisters and a brother. That I once played the clarinet in my school band. I was just a nameless piece of flesh to be used. A piece of shit.

When these freaks climbed on top of me, I learned to close my eyes and think about things. I remembered going to the pool with my friends in the summer and riding my bike to the cornfields. I even remembered some of the dolls and stuffed animals I would play with.

I sometimes thought about how I got into this mess. The stupid decisions I made. So much for my knight in shining armour. He was the one who did this to me. Even a cop told me I brought this on myself. Maybe I did, but he didn't have to rub it in my face. I know I messed up.

My pimp even branded his name on my back like a cow. I wanted to die, but I was always too afraid of what might happen if I did. Is there a hell? Oh God, what did I do? How did things go so wrong? Oh well. I don't have anything more to say. Everything sucks. Nobody cares.'

Sex trafficking goes beyond physical captivity. It strips people of their dignity and self-worth; robs them of their very soul. In this interview with a survivor in New York City, I witnessed her shattered heart and crushed spirit. Like us, she once had dreams and cherished memories.

Restoring that stolen dignity and self-worth is as important as securing freedom. By listening, empathizing, and taking action, we can help survivors reclaim their lives with dignity and hope.

Since my work has exposed me to sex trafficking cases throughout the world, this story illustrates that the problem can be found anywhere throughout our world.

He Risked His Life for Me, a Brothel Girl

Ravi was a college boy who came to the brothel with friends. I could tell he didn't want to be there. He didn't belong in that place.

I was feeling depressed. I sat with my head down. I didn't want anyone to take me that night. I didn't want to be touched.

His two friends quickly picked out girls and went off. Ravi looked at me for a long time. He came up sheepishly and asked if I would go with him. We went to one of the rooms. I laid back and waited. I wanted it over quickly.

He said, 'I don't want to do anything. Those guys would tease me if I didn't go with a girl. I just want to sit with you. Is that okay? I will pay for your time.'

For a long time, we sat together. I started asking questions. He wasn't like the other boys; he looked embarrassed. He was an engineering student. The two other boys were in his class. He said he just wanted to be back in his room studying. It was nice to just talk. After an hour, he left.

A week later, he came back. When I entered the parlour, he asked if we could go together. I was disappointed—I thought he was different. But when we entered the room, he just wanted to talk again.

Ravi started coming twice a week, then more. He would buy three hours of my time. He talked to me about everything—his studies, his family, his fears, his hopes, his dreams. We enjoyed each other. We became friends. It was the first time I laughed in a long time. He was sweet and looked at me like a person, not like what I was.

One day, he told me that he wanted to buy me out of the brothel. He said he loved me. He wanted to marry me. He ran off to the madam before I could stop him.

Why would he want me? Love is not for girls like me.

That night, the madam and a goonda charged into my room. She slapped me hard. 'That boy came to me,' she hissed. 'He wanted to free you. I don't want him here. Boys in love are dangerous to my business.'

Weeks passed, and Ravi never returned. It was over. My happiness was gone. Then, one night, very early in the morning, Ravi came in. He raced up to me and said, 'We need to leave.' Although I was scared, the goondas were not around. I took his hand, and we ran to the staircase. I felt this might be our only chance.

When we reached the street, one of the goondas came running up. He grabbed my arm and started pulling me back inside. Ravi jumped on him. As he wrestled the goonda to the ground, he shouted, 'Run, run, run.' I did.

The police found me. I was taken to this shelter. I stayed here for three months, not knowing what happened to Ravi.

One day, another girl from my old brothel arrived. I asked her what happened that night. She said the boy was stabbed. He was taken away, bleeding badly. She didn't know anything else.

Did he give his life for me? Why would anyone do that? I am nothing. How could someone ever love me? Love is not for people like me.'

This interview took place in New Delhi. It's one of numerous accounts I've heard about young men developing deep feelings for women and girls trapped in the clutches of human trafficking. Typically, when these crushes are identified, these boys are barred from the brothel—as the madam contends, they are bad for business.

Over time, I've come to understand that the human connections that take place within such establishments often transcend the realm of mere sexual encounters. The story of this brave, smitten boy illustrates how love can thrive even in the most hopeless of places—in this case, a brothel nestled within the heart of the red-light district. It is a reminder that we are all worthy of love, whether we believe it or not.

I'm Alive because Someone Dared to Help

'The front gate was left unlocked for the first time. I managed to run away from the brothel. I made it to the shopping area before the pimp caught up to me. He grabbed my arm and pushed me to the ground while hitting me across my face. I tried to break free, but his grip was too strong.

Some men stopped, and it looked as if they were about to stand up for me, but the pimp shouted, 'She is my wife. It's a family matter. She brought this on herself.'

In Bangladesh, no one dares to step in to help a woman if she is receiving a beating from her husband. They feel he has a right to do so.

I screamed over and over, 'He is not my husband. He runs a brothel. I'm trying to escape. Please help me! Please!'

There was a long pause. No one moved or said anything. No one cares about a brothel girl. Not in Dhaka.

I'm going to die, I thought to myself as my heart sank.

Suddenly, an older man from the crowd stepped in between me and the pimp. He looked right at my attacker. The pimp pushed him away. The man came back again. Another man stood beside him. Then another and another. A few women joined the group of protectors. They formed a wall.

The pimp was greatly outnumbered. There was a moment where his eyes indicated that there was nothing more that he could do. He snarled that he'd find me, that I would be sorry. He turned and left.

A young woman in the crowd grabbed my hand. She took me to a shelter where there were other girls who were able to escape.

I'm alive today because some people dared to help me. They saved my life.'

I heard this story while living and working in Bangladesh. The part about husbands being allowed to beat their wives, sadly, is true.

I was once in a shopping area when I saw a man beat his wife to within an inch of her life. As I moved in to help, several men stopped me and explained, 'If you don't want to be seriously hurt today, don't get involved. It is between him and his wife. He has a right to hit her. If you try to help, the crowd will turn on you. Turn away, brother.' I felt helpless.

Additionally, it is an unfortunate reality that within this culture, many regard women involved in prostitution as undeserving of compassion or aid. They perceive these individuals as immoral and are blind to the possibility that they may have been coerced or deceived into such circumstances.

But despite these prevailing cultural and traditional norms, people do occasionally extend a helping hand. For this to happen, one person must be the first to step forward. Others are then reminded of their own inaction and feel compelled to stand with them, as the crowd did with the older man in the story above.

Every human being, regardless of their background, deserves assistance and the fundamental right to live in freedom. Nothing demonstrates more the power of compassion and unity in the face of adversity than the older man who stood up for this young woman—and the people who joined him.

No One Cares

'People need to open their eyes. They can't put their head in the sand.

People like me are being abused. It's everywhere. There are girls like me everywhere. I'm nobody, but I'm human. I should be treated like everyone else. People treat me like garbage. They look down their nose at me. I can see it in their eyes. They think I'm a criminal—a bad girl. I'm not.

I'm a victim. I'm also a survivor. They explained this to me. I didn't know this before. Now I know.

I never chose this work. Never. My pimp made me his property. He told me to do things and I did them. What choice did I have? He was so cruel.

You will never understand. How can you? How can anyone? It just sucks.

You ask me what could have been done to help me. Is that what you are asking?

Someone could have fixed my family. Someone could have seen my pain. Someone could have helped me out before I ran away. That would have prevented this thing from happening to me.

It isn't hard to find girls like me. If the police want to find us, we are easy to find. But they don't try. If they did try, we'd be out of this work. But no one is looking.

What do I do now? Where do I go? Nobody cares. It is sad but true, nobody cares. If they did, I wouldn't be here today.'

This woman had been trafficked from Los Angeles to Atlanta. I met her when she was seventeen years old. Facing family issues, she ran away from home when she was fourteen. A pimp befriended her at a bus station. After grooming her for three weeks, she was forced into prostitution. She was rescued in an FBI raid and sent to the shelter.

During my interview with her at a US shelter, she repeatedly lamented, 'Nobody cares.' But I refuse to accept that as absolute truth. I believe if we amplify her message, share her experiences, and illuminate her pain, people will care. We must maintain faith in humanity's inherent compassion and empathy.

By opening communication channels, listening, and engaging with each other's struggles, we can make a difference. To lose this belief is to surrender hope. Let us become conduits for change, elevating marginalized voices. Together, we can bridge the gap, challenge indifference, and create a society that truly cares. The moment I stop believing this, I will lose hope. I can't do that.

Being a Victim Is Not What Defines Me

'I want to get out of this shelter. I've been here for so many months. I want to get on with my life.

Something bad happened to me. Okay, I get that. I'm happy it's over, but that's not who I am.

Everyone keeps saying I'm a victim. Some call me a survivor. I'm not really sure what that means, but that doesn't define me.

Those horrible things are over, thank God, but I want to forget them.

But everyone keeps talking about it. I wish people would just stop defining me by what happened. Is a person who's been in a car accident defined by that forever? Is a person who gets dumped by a man defined by that?

All I want to do is move on. Help me to do that.

All you people mean well. You want to help, but sympathy is not what I need. I need to figure out what to do next. I need a job. I need to make money. I need to be left alone to live a normal life. My life.

Please ask me what I want. Don't assume you know. You don't.

It's my future. It is my life—not yours to control, but mine.'

I met this twenty-one-year-old woman from Albania in Bangkok. She was deceived by a casual friend into coming to Thailand, where she was forced into prostitution, living in a small apartment with over fifteen other women. After I gained her trust, she agreed to testify against her trafficker in exchange for police protection.

Over the years, I've met hundreds of survivors of various forms of trafficking. I've learned that their needs and recoveries vary greatly. Some are remarkably resilient, ready to embrace life's next chapter without missing a beat. Others bear deep wounds that need years of healing. Some will never recover.

There is no one-size-fits-all approach to helping these people. Each situation is unique, and needs to be treated as such.

From Victim to Rescuer

I came to this border town four months ago. There are two of us. We were both trafficked to India. I spent two years there and Maya spent one year. We were both told that we would have good work. Instead, they put us in brothels.

I can't think back to those times. It hurts too much. I never want to think of what I had to do.

I was rescued and spent four months at a shelter in Kathmandu. My parents didn't want me back. They blamed me for what happened.

I am still angry with that boy who tricked me. I thought he was my friend.

When I heard that I could stop other girls from being tricked and trafficked, I volunteered.

We stand here and wait to see who crosses the border. We are looking for a boy with a girl or with a few girls. If we see someone who might be a victim, we stop them. We ask many questions.

Most times, it is a married couple or a brother and sister or something else, but sometimes, it is a trafficker taking advantage.

When the boy seems scared and the girl doesn't know him well, we separate them. If the story is different, we tell the girl what happened to us. We tell her that we wanted to go to India because we were promised a good job. We tell her that we had hopes for something great. Many of them don't believe us, but we keep talking until they understand.

The border police give us a space. Our NGO taught them about this crime. They understand what we are doing. They sometimes help.

We have stopped traffickers, but we can't do much with them. The boy can't be arrested, he didn't do anything illegal yet, but the police get his name and he is told they will follow up. We both shout at him and tell him he will go to jail.
  Someone will travel back with the girl to her home.
  I had never been to this part of Nepal before we began identifying victims. It is different from the hills. The people are different, and it is much hotter. I don't like it, but I feel good helping.'

I was moved by the courage and determination of these resilient trafficking survivors at the Birgunj border crossing. They worked tirelessly for this NGO, diligently monitoring individuals leaving Nepal to identify potential victims of trafficking. Their stories are a testament to the incredible impact they've had, with inspiring examples of success.

Victim to Teacher

Years ago, I met an extraordinary individual who had endured unimaginable hardships as a victim of trafficking. For four gruelling years, she had been trapped in a brothel in Kolkata, just like countless other girls who were deceitfully lured away from their small villages in northern India. Initially, she had naïvely ventured into the city with hopes of working as a nanny for a wealthy family. Instead, she found herself ensnared in the depths of prostitution.

'That was the moment when I first realized that not everyone could be trusted,' she recalled. Prior to this cruel twist of fate, she had been a diligent student, consistently achieving high grades in all her subjects. From a young age, she had aspired to become a teacher, a beacon of knowledge and inspiration.

Following her rescue, she spent a few months in a shelter, desperately longing to return home. However, upon her arrival, her family rejected and abandoned her due to the societal stigma surrounding her circumstances. It was in this state of despair that she reached out to a distant aunt in Mumbai, a woman who had never married. The aunt opened her doors and heart to her, embracing her as her own daughter.

For several years, she toiled at a local shop, selling sarees to make ends meet. One fortuitous day, an advertisement in the newspaper caught her attention. It offered a course that could help her obtain the equivalent of a high school education. On a whim, she seized the opportunity and enrolled. With determination and resilience, she completed the course and eventually pursued higher education, fulfilling her long-held dream of becoming a teacher.

Throughout her journey, she found solace in the unwavering support of compassionate professors who became her confidants and advocates. 'They believed in me,' she tearfully recalled. Their faith in her abilities rekindled her own dwindling self-belief and propelled her forward.

I encountered this remarkable woman at a human trafficking conference in Mumbai, where I was delivering a presentation. Following my talk, she approached me, compelled to share her story. She told me that although she had never married, she had discovered contentment in her chosen path. She had dedicated herself to teaching history, using her knowledge and experience to empower others. And she had volunteered at a women's centre, extending her compassion to those in need.

One thing she said has resonated within me ever since:

We are all born with the potential to succeed in life. Sometimes, that potential is stolen away from us. In my case, I believed this would be my fate. However, I was fortunate enough to encounter individuals who saw beyond the shame I carried. They recognized my potential and wholeheartedly believed in me, even when I struggled to believe in myself. They embraced me, nurturing my spirit back to its former strength. As a result, I surpassed even my own expectations and reached my full potential.

In my own life, I have been profoundly influenced by mentors who have experienced the depths of despair but emerged triumphant, defying all odds. They embody the resilience of the human spirit and have taught me invaluable lessons. From this extraordinary woman's journey, I have gleaned that even the most broken individuals can be resurrected with compassion and love. A consistent dose of encouragement can work wonders. Each of us has the capacity to contribute to this process; all it requires is an open heart and mind to those in need.

I Never Once Got a Valentine

During my time working for the United Nations, I had the opportunity to interview a young victim of sex trafficking in Pattaya, Thailand. This particular interview, which coincided with Valentine's Day, left an indelible mark on my memory. As I listened to her harrowing story, I couldn't help but notice the tears in her eyes and the enduring sadness etched on her face.

As our conversation, which took place in a coffee shop, drew to a close, she told me how she dreaded Valentine's Day. She recounted how clients would arrive intoxicated, making crude jokes about the day's significance and expecting her to fulfil their twisted notions of something 'special.'

Moved by her words, I responded with genuine empathy, saying, 'That must have been incredibly difficult for you.'

Pausing to gather her thoughts, she replied, 'Yes, but not for the reasons you might expect.'

With a mix of sorrow and resignation, she explained that unlike her friends back in her village, she had never experienced the simple joys of Valentine's Day. She lamented how everything that most people took for granted—the first Valentine's card, the first date, the first rose, the first time holding hands, the first kiss, the first dance, and even the first boyfriend—had all been stolen from her.

This exchange left me with a deep sense of helplessness. I yearned to do something meaningful for her on that day, but I struggled to find a way. What could I possibly do?

Victims of trafficking are denied the pleasure of receiving cards, indulging in chocolates, enjoying romantic dinners, and cherishing tender moments. Their lives and their right to experience things the rest of us take for granted—the beauty of tradition, celebration, and joyful occasions—have been cruelly stolen from them.

This young woman's story highlighted just one aspect of the many injustices inflicted upon the victims of human trafficking. It was a stark reminder of the depth of their suffering and the urgency of our battle.

Please Listen to Me, I Have Something to Say

Each and every one of the resilient women and girls I met had their own hopes and dreams. Here are some of them:

Sushma aspired to become a teacher. When I spoke with her in Nepal, she radiated excitement while recounting her favourite teacher's influence, who inspired her to create art and write.

Pari longed to have a family of her own. She fondly described her family's farm, which overlooked the breathtaking Annapurna Mountain range in Nepal. To her, home was one of the most beautiful places on earth. Having visited it many times, I had to agree.

Despite being banished by her family following her trafficking ordeal, Prachi yearned for the impossible—to reunite her entire family once more. Though doubtful, her dream persisted.

For Sanjita, a simple desire burned within her—to be loved by someone, just one person.

Maya expressed her wish for her story to be shared to aid others. When I informed her about another trafficking survivor who traversed the Nepalese hills to spread awareness, she became excited, proclaiming, 'That's exactly what I'll do for the rest of my life.'

Zara's dream was to receive her mother's forgiveness for what she had endured. Even when reassured that it wasn't her fault, she replied with a heavy burden of self-blame, 'There must have been something in my past that brought this upon me. It was my fault.'

Nima yearned to find a man who would accept her past unconditionally and love her despite her background.

Rekha simply wished for the tormenting fear she experienced to dissipate. Each touch from another person sent crippling shockwaves through her entire body.

Mina spoke of her craving for the flavours of village food. She vividly described her mother's unparalleled culinary skills.

Each of these stories remains emblazoned in my memory, their faces eternally imprinted in my mind. Each one of them deserves to be heard.

However, mere acknowledgment is not enough. If we listen to their harrowing tales without taking action to prevent such atrocities, we become complicit in the problem.

Behind every sex trafficking victim lies a childhood, a family, a home, and a personal history. They, too, know love. They harbour dreams. They yearn for affection. Their hopes are the same as our hopes.

Victim to Hero

'I don't care what you say, I'm going to go out and talk to the people in Nepal. They need to understand about traffickers. They have to know what to do to protect their families. They need to stop this from happening. Someone has to do it. Let it be me. I have nothing left to lose. It is time that someone acts. I can't just sit here and let it happen.'

During my early counter-trafficking years in Nepal, I met a girl named Heena who offered this testimonial. She had just returned from the brothels in India.

Heena had been trafficked when she was only fourteen into one of the most notorious sex establishments. She spent three gruelling years there before being rescued. During our interview, she talked about the terrible rapes, torture, and abuse she endured daily. She suffered from a range of sexually transmitted diseases, including AIDS.

After six weeks in one of the local shelters, her anger continued to grow. On a number of occasions, she vowed to the shelter staff that she would travel into the northern villages, which had produced many victims, in order to share her story. She said she was determined to prevent any more Nepalese girls from ever experiencing the same terrible ordeal she had endured.

Several counsellors tried to talk Heena out of her decision. They warned that a young girl shouldn't be travelling alone in the hills of Nepal. They cautioned that her health would continue to worsen.

But it was clear that nothing was going to get in her way. Realizing that we couldn't change her mind, we asked if she'd agree to travel with a companion. After much persuasion, she finally allowed a male social worker to accompany her.

Over a six-month period, Heena travelled throughout Nepal, telling her story. In each village, she'd locate the centre square where she'd sit down and begin recounting her story. At first, there would be five or six people listening. Then others would join. At the end, many of the villagers appeared shocked and horrified by her emotional testimony. Others cried when they heard the fate of so many young girls.

At the end of each talk, someone would inevitably raise their hand and say, 'What can we do to protect our young girls?' At this point, the social worker would say, 'I am glad you asked that question. Down the road, at another village, we talked about this and came up with a plan to start a neighbourhood watch. At the village before that, they decided to put in place a school registration system.'

The best part about this approach was that solutions were identified on the spot. Many suggestions could be put in place with little or no effort. The community's participation in the process ensured that the suggestions remained relevant to their own cultural and traditional needs.

Heena's courage helped prevent others from experiencing her fate. She continued her travels until she grew too sick to go on. There are many heroes in the fight against this crime—Heena was one of them.

2

Slave Labour

Labour trafficking devastates lives, rips families apart, and ensnares countless men, women, and children in a web of deceit, manipulation, and false promises. These people are stolen, lured, or coerced into non-existent opportunities, only to find themselves trapped in a merciless cycle of enslavement and exploitation.

The following stories are meant to illustrate the many faces of this heinous crime; to undermine the misconception that it affects only the impoverished, or uneducated, or those from less developed countries. These stories are also meant to shed light on the profound human suffering traffickers inflict and the compassion of those striving to bring healing and redemption.

If You Don't Do What I Say, I Will Hurt Your Family

'After arriving at the factory, one of the first things I was shown was a short video on a mobile phone of a young man being beaten to death with a club. When I tried to turn away, they held my head in place to force me to watch the video till the end. I still remember all the blood. I was told that if I ever tried to run, this would happen to me and my family members. From that point on, I did everything they said.'

I met this man at an NGO office in Thailand. After fleeing the violence in Myanmar, he secured employment at a small seafood packing company. Once there, he was forced to toil in this sweatshop for more than four years. Within a few hours of arriving, he was exposed to this violent content.

Most people can't understand why human trafficking victims don't just run away. Many of them are not chained or locked in place, so why don't they just run off? Often, the answer lies in the threats they receive.

If someone said to you, 'Do what I say, or I will hurt your mother and father,' how could you ignore it?

I have heard these kinds of threats time and time again. The fear they create can be so extreme that even years after a person has escaped their trafficker, they still experience post-traumatic stress disorder (PTSD).

The chains are not on a victim's hands or feet; they are in a person's mind.

The Neighbour's Children Saved My Life

'My family was tricked by a trafficker and promised that I'd be working as a nanny in a big house in Mumbai. When I got to my new workplace, it was something much different—they made me into a slave. I worked from 5 a.m. until midnight every day for three years. I never had a day off or any time to rest. I was never paid.

If I didn't work hard enough, I was hit with a shoe. Food was taken away from me. I couldn't call or talk with anyone, including my family. No one knew where I was living.

The property had a high wall around it with locked doors at the entrance; there was no way I could have escaped.

One day, I heard children playing in the street. I was desperate to escape, so I put a note in a plastic bottle and threw it over the wall. It explained my situation and included a plea for help. All at once, they went quiet.

For three days, I waited; nothing happened. Then on the fourth day, a policeman came. While my employer tried to say there was no problem, I ran up to the officer and begged for help. He took me away to the station. I was rescued.

If I hadn't thrown that bottle, I would still have been there today.'

When I met this resilient young woman, she was twenty-one. Throughout our conversation, her body trembled with enduring trauma, tears tracing a heartbreaking path down her cheeks. Even after the passage of three long years, her wounds remained evident.

Her story is testament to the determined spirit of trafficked victims and their tenacious pursuit of freedom. The courage and resourcefulness of this remarkable young woman were rewarded. Reunited with her family, she was able to find happiness in her life again.

Since That Day, I've Been Afraid of the Police

'My first memory? I was a very young boy when I came to Kolkata. It was a big mistake. I was playing in an empty train carriage with my friends. Suddenly, the train left the station. My friends were older. They jumped off. I couldn't do it, I was too afraid.

Hours later, the train arrived at the main station. It took me a long time to leave the train. I cried. I finally got up and entered the busy station. There were so many people. Everyone was walking fast. I didn't know what to do.

A man came up to me and asked where my parents were. I told him what happened. He took my hand, and we left the station. He said he was taking me to them. I was then put into a car with two other boys. After a long ride, we drove to a large compound that had high brick walls. Inside were a few mud huts. The space was filled with old bricks.

Every day, I had to sit in front of a collection of bricks. My job was to take the hammer and crush them into smaller pieces. There were nine of us doing this. We ate two meals a day—rice and dal. We worked from early morning until late at night. If we talked, we were beaten. If we didn't work fast enough, we were beaten. Even if we did our work, they beat us.

One day, the guard got drunk. He passed out. One of the boys went up to him, grabbed the key, and we managed to escape. As we were leaving the compound, one of the other adults saw us and started running after us. We ran for our lives. Just as he was about to catch up with us, we saw a policeman. We ran up to him, wrapped our arms around him, and shouted. We pointed back at the man who was chasing us.

We were taken to a police car. The three of us sat in the back seat. The policeman drove to a public pay phone and talked with someone for a long time. When he came back to us, he said he was taking us to a police station.

The ride only lasted a few minutes. It ended in front of the compound we had escaped from. Upon our arrival, the guards pulled us out, took us inside, and beat us. They handed the policeman a package. One of the boys nearly died from this beating.

It took another two years before a group of people rescued us. We were taken to a shelter and then placed in the care of some nice people. I am now going to school.

But since that day, I am afraid of the police. To me, they are as bad as the men who held us. How could that man do that to us? He was supposed to help people. Why didn't he help me?'

When I interviewed this boy, he had already turned nine. Sadly, what he experienced is all too common. Traffickers often lurk in the shadows of train and bus stations, preying upon the vulnerable, employing violence and insidious threats to shackle these innocent souls in their wicked grasp. This is how childhoods are stolen.

I Can't Stop Feeling Angry

'I was seventeen years old when I was put on that fishing boat. They said I'd only be on the boat for four months. But we stayed out for over three years. There were three men from Myanmar and two from Cambodia. The captain was Thai. He had two others that were Thai.

From that first day, we were abused. They hit us, shouted at us, and took away food if we didn't do the work. When the fish were there, we worked continuously without sleep. I was always exhausted. Even when I was given time to sleep I couldn't. I was too scared. I dreamed about fishing and being beaten. The nightmares stayed.

One of the men from Cambodia hurt his hand badly. It was crushed and turned blue. He couldn't work. When I woke up the next day, he wasn't there. They threw him in the ocean. When the collection boat arrived, another man was put on our boat. No one talked about what happened to that man. We all knew it could happen to us too.

The captain had a pistol. When he got drunk, he would take it out and show us. Sometimes he'd shoot in the air. He wanted us to know he would use it.

There was another boy. Sometimes the captain would take him to his cabin. That boy had it much worse than me. We never talked about what happened in that room. We all knew.

I made a bad choice. I regret agreeing to go on that boat. During one of our trips, we came close to shore. I couldn't take it any more. When no one was looking, I jumped into the ocean and swam. It took me hours, but I made it to shore. I was in Malaysia. A man on the beach saw me swimming. He took me to the police. They said others like me made it to shore. Some others drown.

Some people in Malaysia helped me to get to the capital. Two weeks later, I was back in Cambodia. Even after all this time, I am angry—angry for agreeing to go on that boat, angry for what they did to me, and angry that more people like me are going on those boats.

You asked me what needs to happen. People in the villages need to know about this. Thailand is filled with traps. Don't go there. Don't think that things will be better. They will not. There are bad people. People who hurt other people. I didn't know this. Now I do. I'll never go back to that country. Never.'

This was an interview I did in Cambodia. This young man has PTSD. He was so traumatized by the experience, he couldn't work. His hands trembled throughout the interview.

It Can Happen to Anyone

Below is an email exchange while I was working at the United Nations in Thailand that opened my eyes to the fact that trafficking can happen to anyone.

Victim: *I am an Australian male here in Thailand. I'm a twenty-four-year-old graduate. I think I've been trafficked. Can you help?*

Me: *Are you okay? Can you provide some details?*

Victim: *No, I'm not okay. I'm freaked out and f**king scared. I took a job in Phuket. I have a degree in computer science. I was hired by a small* *wholesale company to set up their website and do their data work. I wanted to experience Thailand, so I took the job. They said I needed a motorcycle to get around. They gave it to me, and I used it to get back and forth to work. I didn't like the job from the beginning. They made me work nearly every day until midnight. When I told them that I wanted to quit, things went bad. They said I owed them AUD 5,000 for the motorcycle. They said I agreed to buy it. This wasn't true, and motorbikes don't cost that much. Since they had my passport, I couldn't leave. They said it was lost. When I said I was going to go to the police, they asked me if I loved my family. They said if I do that, something bad would happen to them in Australia.*

Me: *I'm very sorry to hear this. Can you give us details about your location? Who these people are?*

Victim: *Can you protect me? Can you protect my family?*

Me: *We will do everything we can to protect you. The police will go to the business and investigate your claims. What you describe sounds like a trafficking case. You will be given support by the government and NGOs. The business owner will be arrested.*

Victim: *What about my family in Australia?*

Me: *Have you been able to communicate with them? Do they know what is happening?*

Victim: *No. They said my family would be hurt if I tried to contact the police or my family.*

Me: *We understand your concerns. We want to find a way to help you. Can we talk on the phone? If you think they are tracking your phone, can you buy another SIM card and call? Here is my number: ***.*

Regrettably, I never received a response from him. With no further information to guide us, the case grew cold. I reached out to someone from the Australian Embassy, but even they felt there was insufficient evidence to proceed with the case.

This account—and many others like this that I have encountered—serves as a stark reminder that human traffickers can victimize anyone. They do not come only for the impoverished, uneducated, or vulnerable individuals from less developed countries. They are a scourge against us all.

A Slave to Construction

'When I arrived at the construction site, I was so excited to have a job. The foreman promised me a stable salary. Even though he said he couldn't pay me for the first three months, I didn't mind. I trusted him. I called my mom and dad and cried; I was so happy that I finally found a job. I had given up hope of finding work. They were so proud of me.

Every day I worked from 7 a.m. to 7 p.m. There was seldom time to eat. The work was hard and dangerous, but I felt grateful that I had a job.

After three months, I went to get my pay, but the foreman told me that I'd have to wait another two months. I was upset, but I didn't have any other options. What else could I do? I had already borrowed a lot of money; I couldn't borrow any more. I felt even more burdened and anxious.

I found someone else to lend me more money. But each time I asked the foreman for my wages, I was told the same answer—next month, next month, next month. I couldn't sleep most nights, I was so worried.

After twelve months passed, I was desperate. I was heavily in debt, without any money. When I heard there were others like me, we all got together, and as a group, we approached the foreman. He was so angry.

The next day, an immigration van pulled up and the police took us all away. They treated us like we were bad men. We weren't criminals, we were just there to work for pay.

The foreman stood there and smiled. He called the police. I could tell that he had never planned to pay any of us. How did I not see this coming?

In two weeks, I was deported. For an entire year, I worked for nothing. For an entire year, I was a slave.

What am I going to tell my parents? How can I face them with nothing? I didn't know. I didn't know. And I have so much debt. I don't know what to do.'

This is the account of a trafficking victim from Laos who fell prey to exploitation in Thailand's construction industry. Such scams, that target vulnerable migrants, are a form of modern-day slavery—and they plague construction sites across the world.

How a $20 Debt Can Ruin a Family

Getting a person into a slavery-like situation through debt is easy. When I lived and worked in Bangladesh, I often saw people entering forced labour and slavery conditions for less than $20.

The scenario went something like this: A rickshaw driver earns no more than $5 per day. He and his family live from hand to mouth, using this limited money to cover their food and housing in the slums. At the end of the day, there is never anything left. They have no savings.

Then one day, a family member becomes very ill. To save this person's life, the family needs $20 to buy medicines. With no savings to fall back on, they borrow the money from a loan shark at an alarmingly high rate of interest. In some cases, this could be over 400 per cent.

But since this family will never earn more than $5 per day, and because this money is needed to survive, they will never be able to pay back both the loan and the interest.

To recover his loan, the moneylender may insist that a family member be taken away to work for a duration of time to pay off this debt. This could be the spouse or a child. With excessive interest, this could take a year or more. The moneylender could also force the rickshaw driver to work part-time for him for many years without any pay.

This process is called debt bondage, and it creates a lasting exploitative connection between the moneylender and the victim.

I Lost Three Years of My Life

'Our village was attacked by the government soldiers. I escaped from Myanmar to Thailand with nothing but my life. I needed to support myself, but I didn't know how. Finally, I heard that there were many small factories that offered work along the ocean peeling shrimp, so I travelled there. I didn't know which one had work to offer, so I just chose one.

I was twenty-one then. The man who managed the factory said I could have a job. We negotiated a salary of 1,500 Baht ($50 a month), but he said I couldn't leave the factory.

I had never made so much money in a month. I was very happy with the offer. I needed to survive, so I agreed to not leave.

After working fifteen hours a day for nearly two months under terrible conditions—watery rice and a concrete floor to sleep on—I went to the manager and asked for my pay. He smiled and laughed before saying, 'I am sorry, I forgot to mention that it costs me 1,700 Baht ($54 a month) to keep you here with food and board, but I am only paying you 1,500 Baht ($50 a month). Now you owe me money. Until you pay it back, you cannot leave this place.'

The more I worked, the more debt I owed. With so much work with nothing in return, my heart was filled with hopelessness and despair. For three years, I was not able to leave. No one could. With armed guards, barbed wire, and high walls, we couldn't escape.

They would sometimes take a worker who was protesting to the back and beat him until he was bloody. They would then show us pictures taken on their phone and threaten us by saying, 'If you try to leave, this will happen to you and your family.' I believed them. I was so filled with regret and sorrow for taking this job.

Suddenly, the police raided the factory, and we were all freed. If they hadn't come, I would never have been able to leave. I lost three years of my life. Gone . . . stolen.'

This story is from a Myanmar trafficking victim who was exploited in Thailand.

Shipbreaking

'I began working at this place four years ago. They made me work here. I owed money after a cyclone destroyed my home and I had to pay it back. My debt was managed by the yard manager.

I work from 6 a.m. to 8 p.m.—sometimes longer. I work every day. Because of my debt, I don't get paid. They give me food and a place to sleep only. They keep telling me that I owe more money. They never tell me how much.

The ships come from all over. Big ships.

They take the ships, get them going at full speed, and then they hit the coast. The company people then begin to break the ships into small pieces. I am one of the workers who carry the heavy metal away to the loading area.

Look at me. I don't have any protective clothing or shoes to wear. I've lost two of my fingers.

I also have a cough that doesn't go away. It's from the bad air. The work is very dangerous. Some of my friends have also been hurt. Some badly. I have seen people killed from explosions and having ship parts fall on them.

This is the last place in Bangladesh for workers. It is the lowest kind of work. Most do this because they have no other options. I do it because I must. The debt.

I think I might die here. I don't really care any more. My life is nothing but this awful work.'

During my time in Bangladesh, I visited the Chittagong Ship Breaking Yard three times. It was a chilling experience that I'll never forget. From the moment you enter this area, everything feels dangerous. I witnessed huge parts of ships that were ten storeys tall falling to the ground. One of them nearly hit us. The very atmosphere seemed laden with a noxious concoction of chemical odours, an inescapable haze that clung to our senses.

The interview cited above offers a glimpse into the life of a worker, a forlorn figure cloaked in a film of grease and grime. His eyes spoke volumes, reflecting a sense of desolation that words alone could not convey.

Such places exist in various corners of the world, where employment becomes an act of last resort. In these grim domains, peril, disease, and despondency converge to create a breeding ground for human exploitation. Here, hope languishes, replaced by an abyss of hopelessness. It represents the ultimate juncture, where the thread of opportunity unravels, leaving behind a stark void that resonates with despair.

At Sea, Nobody Can Hear You Scream

'I was sixteen years old when I was tricked onto that fishing boat. My friend said the work would be easy and that I'd be paid a good wage. I thought the boat would only stay out for a few months, but it stayed out for three years.

The work never stopped. When the fish were running, we were up for days at a time. Even when they weren't running, we worked eighteen hours. I was so tired sometimes that I felt I'd go crazy.

If they thought I wasn't working hard enough, they'd beat me. Even when I didn't do anything wrong, I was hit with a stick. I was afraid of the captain. He was so cruel. For food, we ate nothing but fish and rice twice a day. After two years of this, I began to feel weak all the time, but even if I got sick or injured, I worked.

I had seen others who had been seriously injured, and the captain simply threw them over the side of the boat. I still remember their pleas for help as the ocean carried them away to their death. To keep me working, they would force me to take powerful drugs that destroyed my body.

When I finally returned to the port after years at sea, I was not given any pay. The captain told me that I was an illegal migrant, so he didn't have to give me anything.

Having no way to communicate with my family while I was away, my mother and father assumed I was dead. Since they moved away, I don't know how to find them.'

I interviewed this man in Cambodia, several years after he had made it back to dry land. To prevent others from being trafficked, he was participating in a Khmer documentary film project to teach potential victims how to protect themselves from would-be traffickers. But he never fully recovered from his own ordeal.

A New Form of Human Trafficking

'I thought I was going to get a good job in Cambodia. The online advertisement said I'd make $3,000 per month. That is so much money. After I did a short online interview with them, I was offered a job in a casino. I was happy. I could never find a job like this in Taiwan, so I took it.

After arriving, some men took me in a van to a building in the city. It had high walls and barbed wire all around. They began shouting at me. Every day they made me sit in front of a computer and scam people for their money for *fourteen hours. I felt bad. These were just ordinary people, but I had to do it. If I didn't earn enough money, they would take me to a room and hit me with bats or electric tasers. I thought they were going to kill me.*

There were others like me there from all over Asia. Hundreds of us. We were all forced to do this work.

I found a way to contact my family. To let me leave, my family had to pay $30,000. They didn't know if I'd be freed, but I was let go.'

In recent times, an alarming and sinister form of human trafficking has emerged that demands our unwavering attention. Criminal syndicates in Asia have adopted a chillingly innovative approach, one that ensnares individuals into a vicious cycle of scamming others.

This takes shape through two predominant methods. Victims are either lured under the false pretence of a lucrative job opportunity or ensnared by online romantic entanglements that coerce them to relocate to Southeast Asia. Once there, they are imprisoned and forced to take part in scamming others. Those who resist often find themselves subjected to severe physical abuse and torture. I have witnessed harrowing footages depicting the brutal methods including electrocutions with tasers, beatings, and sexual abuse employed to punish these hapless victims.

People from Hong Kong, Taiwan, Thailand, Cambodia, Vietnam, and far beyond have been deceived and abducted, finding themselves prisoners in these scam facilities scattered across Cambodia and Myanmar. There are reports of similar facilities operating in Nepal, Laos, and Dubai, a chilling warning of how this practice, if left unchecked, could spread in the months and years to come.

Once confined to these fraud centres, the victims are trained to execute a scam called 'pig butchering', in which they romance other victims online with a motive to cheat them out of their money. The term 'pig butchering' refers to a heavily scripted, and contact-intensive process to fatten up the prey before slaughter. This scam is predominately executed by a ring of cryptocurrency scammers who mine dating apps and social media sites for victims. It involves a scammer creating a fake profile used to reach out to victims often through social media, WhatsApp, or dating sites.

The goal is to initiate a discussion with the victim, attempting to be their new friend or lover. The new friend creates reasons to continue a conversation, which leads to multiple calls. They slowly develop a relationship.

While building trust with the victim, they introduce the idea of making a business investment using cryptocurrency. The scammer employs persuasion rather than requesting money outright because they are aware that individuals are savvy and know that being asked for money by a stranger is a sign of a potential scam.

The victim is drawn into what appears to be a benign talk about cryptocurrency investments, but they are really being manipulated to make an investment. The new friend convinces the target to invest in cryptocurrency and refers them to a bogus website that looks authentic but is controlled by the scammer. The victims are encouraged to invest small amounts in the beginning and the scammer will make sure to post a modest gain on the investment. They may even allow the victim to withdraw money to convince them the process is legitimate.

The victim is then persuaded to invest larger amounts. Once the money is sent to the fake investment app, the scammer vanishes.

In addition, there are other approaches which involve the scammer posing as a customer service representative, tech support agent, or in another role. Scammers may use phone calls, emails, or online messages to target unsuspecting people around the world.

The scams often employ social engineering tactics, preying on emotions like fear or trust. For instance, perpetrators might impersonate government officials, law enforcement officers, or tech support personnel, claiming urgent issues that require immediate action or payment. They exploit the victim's lack of information and create a sense of urgency, coercing them into providing sensitive personal or financial information.

Cryptocurrency has become an increasingly prevalent element in these scams. Perpetrators may manipulate victims into making payments using cryptocurrencies, leveraging the pseudonymous and decentralized nature of these digital assets to obfuscate their identities and evade law enforcement. The use of cryptocurrency adds an additional layer of complexity to tracking and apprehending those behind such scams, as traditional financial institutions are not involved in these transactions, making it challenging to follow the money trail. The proceeds from these scams are typically funnelled back into the criminal organizations orchestrating them through cryptocurrency channels, further complicating efforts to trace and apprehend the individuals involved.

* * *

The stories in the first two chapters illustrate how human trafficking preys upon the vulnerable and violates the fundamental rights of individuals.

Hearing the unimaginable horrors these people have endured is not easy but is essential if we are to have any hope of ending this scourge. Putting a human face on the statistics helps us to understand the physical, emotional, spiritual, and psychological traumas inflicted and forces us to recognize the urgency of the situation.

Telling these stories also empowers the survivors. Their narratives shed light on the human capacity for survival, resilience, and the potential for healing. By sharing their experiences, survivors reclaim their voices, often becoming advocates for change.

When I hear their stories, I feel compelled to help. I hope you feel the same.

3

The Traffickers' Tale

As I said earlier, the foremost experts on modern slavery are not people like me, but those with first-hand experience of living in this dark and horrible world. That means not only the victims who have endured its horrors, but those at whose hands they suffer: the traffickers.

As someone who has dedicated more than thirty-five years to combating modern slavery, I never cease to be confounded by the cold, calculating, and evil nature of traffickers. I often find myself pondering the catalysts that led these individuals astray, questioning the experiences or circumstances that could drive someone down such a morally bankrupt path.

Below are testimonials from traffickers that shed light on the motives, methods, and networks they employ, as well as the psychological factors that drive their actions.

If the Girl is Pretty, We Can Sell Her For a Lot of Money

'Sometimes we use veteran prostitutes as bait. They know what to say to win over the young girls. We hire a man to pretend to be her husband. Then, we rent them a small house for a few days.

While living in that house, the prostitute becomes friendly with the community, particularly with the young girls. Then one day our prostitute asks one of the girls if she would like to go out with her to a movie or to a park.

Most parents don't allow young girls to go out except to school, but if it is with another woman, it is not a problem.

She then takes the girl to the brothel. As soon as she arrives there, the girl is surrounded, and it is too late for her. Among this crowd, there are teenage boys.

They start teasing and touching her until they ultimately rape her as an initiation into the trade. Once spoiled, her community will not accept her back, and she belongs to us.

If the girl is pretty, we can earn a lot of money. Sometimes we can get one or two girls this way before the community gets clever. Then we just move on.'

During my time in Bangladesh, our partners were given access to human traffickers who were in prison. This is one of the stories told to them.

The NGO worker who interviewed this man described how excited the criminal became when he talked about this wicked process. His eyes opened wide, his hand gestures increased, and his voice got much louder. He said that this imprisoned trafficker appeared to take pride in the creative way he was able to manipulate and deceive his victims.

I asked if he appeared to have any remorse. The interviewer said no. His only regret was that he got caught.

Catch Me If You Can

Years ago, I was in Hanoi and received a call from a local Vietnamese man. He asked if I was Matthew Friedman. I said yes. He then asked if he could meet with me. As a UN official, I used to get these kinds of calls regularly. It was often someone who wanted to better understand the nature of my work.

The next day, we met in a small café. He was well-dressed and well-educated. In fact, I'd go as far as saying that he was very interesting and pleasant. For an hour, I talked about my work.

When I finished, I asked, 'So, what do you do?'

Without hesitation, he said, 'I'm a human trafficker.' I was shocked. He went on to state that he always wanted to talk to someone like me and thanked me for my time.

While part of me wanted to storm off, I decided instead to continue talking to him. For the next hour, he described how he trafficked women and girls into forced prostitution and sometimes men into forced labour. I was surprised by how open he was. He didn't hold anything back. At one point, he handed me his business card and said, 'Go ahead and try to catch me. You'll never be able to. I'm too insulated.'

He began by saying my work was a joke. He said, as a criminal, he had the ability to change his approach, if necessary, to keep ahead of the game. He said that in my NGO world, we followed static plans and inflexible procedures. He was right. Because we had to abide by rules, he felt we'd never win the fight. He said that in his world, they had no rules. They could be unethical, unconventional, unorthodox, and ruthless. He said this was the reason why crime paid. The legal system was too encumbered by processes and procedures that constantly tripped it up. He laughed, repeatedly.

He added that the NGOs and the United Nations were not equipped to do counter-trafficking work; they didn't understand the criminal world and without understanding it, they could do little to stop it.

He said that greed was always a much more efficient motivator than the desire to save the world. In his case, the outcome of his work was a handful of cash. It was tangible and real and offered instant gratification. In my case, the profit was 'a person gets helped'. Properly helping a person is anything but quick or easy.

His narcissism and excessive bravado were grotesque, and only inspired me to up my game and work even harder to go after people like this.

There will come a day when traffickers feel vulnerable. When it does, I hope I get to meet this man again.

It Is Like Having an ATM Machine

'We started trafficking people into scam centres during COVID. We thought we could hire people to scam others but people from these countries don't like to do this kind of work. Even if we provided them with a lot of money, they just don't want to do it. I don't understand why.

Having a person scam is like having an ATM machine. They just keep getting more and more money for us. It is a great way to get rich.

I still don't understand why these people don't just accept the work. They could get good money too. But they resist. They make me force them to work. If I hit them or taser them a few times, it is a great motivating approach. It would be easier if I didn't have to do this. But this is what needs to be done. It is just part of the business. You know what I'm talking about. We can't have them say no to us.'

This testimonial came from a person who was involved in trafficking young Asians from across the region into scam centres in Myanmar. He left the business when he thought he might get caught in a police raid.

* * *

The stories above are meant to give a perspective on trafficking beyond that which can be gleaned from external observers, academic studies, or even victim accounts. The stories of the traffickers themselves give us insights into the inner workings of this crime and the motivations that drive them.

Often, their stories go against our preconceived notions. They should challenge us to confront some uncomfortable truths about human behaviour, societal vulnerabilities, and systemic failures that enable this crime to continue.

4

Perspectives

Human trafficking affects lives beyond those of the traffickers and those they trafficked. Mothers and fathers, sons and daughters, neighbours and colleagues—all these people are affected in their own unique ways. Their stories, too, deserve to be heard.

Three Angry Women

'*One afternoon, me and two of my co-workers, all women, were having lunch together in our company cafeteria.*

At the next table, Brian, one of the young sales reps, was bragging to his friends that he had had sex with three different teenage prostitutes in Bangkok on a recent holiday trip. In a loud voice, he said, 'It's like being back in high school again. They are so young and beautiful. For forty bucks you can have a girl for an hour.'

The other men hung on to every one of his words. We all looked at each other with sheer disgust. After his friends left, the three of us walked over to Brian's table and sat down with him. What he said was so offensive, we had to say something. Brian appeared shocked to be facing three angry middle-aged mothers. There was a long pause.

Susan, the alpha of our group, said to him with a measured rage in her voice, 'We couldn't help but overhear what you said about being with teenage girls in Thailand.'

He squirmed in his chair. He was busted.

'Brian, do you have any sisters?' she asked. He nodded.

'Do you remember when she was sixteen?'

He didn't respond.

'Would it be right for her at sixteen to be with a twenty-five-year-old man?'

He remained silent.

'What you did is not only morally repugnant but also illegal. Having sex with a minor is a criminal offence. It doesn't matter if it happens here or there. Do you understand what I'm saying?'

Brian continued to look terrified.

'Would it be okay for us to share your holiday stories with everyone in the company? You seemed so proud of them a few minutes ago with your friends. Can we help you get the word out?'

He shook his head.

'If we had proof that you did these things, we would have gone to your supervisor. But since you could just be a stupid man bragging for the sake of bragging, we won't. But if we hear this mentioned again, we are going to make sure that everyone in the company learns about your crimes, and if we hear you're going to travel to a foreign country again for any reason, we are going to find you and remind you of this little talk. You hear me?'

His head remained lowered. He knew what he did was wrong. We could all feel his shame and embarrassment.'

I heard this story from a woman who worked for a retail company in the Midwestern US. One summer, they asked me to make a presentation on modern slavery for their 560 employees.

I asked if she thought their stern lecture would make a difference in Brian's life.

She paused for a moment and then said, 'I don't know for sure. We felt so angry and had to call him out. But you know something, there are few things in life scarier than three angry women.'

I Lost My Daughter for Two Years

My daughter answered an ad in the newspaper. They wanted women to go to Japan to work in a restaurant. They didn't need to do anything but send a photo and sign some papers.

She asked me about this. I said no. I said people outside of Mongolia can't be trusted, that there would be no family there to protect her, but she went anyway. I only found out after she left.

For two weeks, she was in Japan. She wrote to me about the city. She said the work was hard, but she liked being in a new place. Two weeks later, she said she was going to Macau. They needed someone to fill in at a casino café.

After that, I didn't hear anything from her. She stopped sending messages. I tried to contact the agency, but they weren't there any more. I didn't know where the restaurant was.

One day, eighteen months after she disappeared, I received an email: 'I'm in trouble. I can't leave. I need help. Still in Macau.' I went to the police. They said they couldn't help me. Someone said to talk to a reporter who knew about girls in Macau. When I got there, I learned the truth—how girls are tricked into leaving Mongolia and then forced into prostitution in Macau.

When I learned this, I went to the United Nations in Ulaanbaatar. They told me they couldn't help me; they didn't deal with individual cases. I went to another agency, and they said they didn't deal with international cases. I went to another NGO, and they said that they only focused on forced labour cases.

No one had an answer for me. The government people said the same thing. For nearly a year, I tried to get my daughter back. No one helped me. I wanted to go to Macau, but I didn't have the money. I didn't know what to do.

Six months later, my daughter came back. I don't know why they let her go, but she was different. She didn't talk about what she had to do, but I knew everything, and I knew why she didn't talk. She didn't want to bring shame to our home. Her spirit was completely gone. All I can do is cry for her.

I don't know why there are so many groups who say that they work on this problem that don't really do anything at all. If they work on this problem, they should find a way to help. They shouldn't say they do this if they don't.

We couldn't do anything to arrest these 'dogs' who did this to my daughter. They are slippery eels; they can't be caught. But if I ever find them, I'll stab them right in the heart.'

I interviewed this woman during one of my trips to Mongolia. Based on this story, an NGO developed a hotline to protect women from being tricked into this situation. This programme helped to bring multiple organizations together to fight the problem. I raised the money for this from the Canadian government.

I Grew Up in a Brothel with My Mother

I don't remember much about when I was small. I spent a lot of it under my mother's bed. When you are a boy in this place, nobody wants you running around. I was often given pills to make me sleep. I slept a lot.

As a child, I did not understand what was happening in this place. I only found out many years later.

I didn't care what my mother did. She was my mother. There was no shame in my world. Everyone understood the world. I only felt shame when I was outside. Everyone told me I should feel shame.

I never talked about where I lived or what my mother did. She had no choice. They made her do this. Even when she could leave, there was no place to go.

I tried to be a goonda, but I was too small, and I couldn't be mean to the ladies. Many of them were there when I grew up. They would give me food and soda. I ran errands for them. They were all my big sisters.

When I was small, I was told to fear the men who came into the brothel. My mother would say that some of them were bad men who would do bad things to me. This never happened to me, but I heard it happened to others.

I was in school for a few years, but I dropped out. I didn't like school. I was different from the other kids.

I started selling liquor to customers when I was eleven. I made good money. Many of them were drunk and didn't mind paying more. They wanted to impress the girls.

People sometimes ask me if I feel bad about my life. I don't. My mother did what she could. I now support myself. Who can pick their own life? No one. I do what I can.

My mother died from the disease. It happened quickly. She got a bad cough, and she was gone three months later. I don't have any other family. Who could know their father in a place like that?

I am alone. Just me. I now sell tea at a local government building. I like the work. They treat me good.

I want to marry someday. I don't know how to do this. Who wants to marry a person who has no family? How would I explain what happened to me? Maybe I'll marry a girl from the brothel. They understand me. They understand where I come from. They understand my old world.'

I interviewed this young man in his early twenties at a shelter in Kolkata. He was visiting one of the girls, and my chance encounter with him provided me with a unique perspective on life in the red-light district.

Despite the immense challenges and hardships faced by those exposed to the extremes of brothel life, some people manage to overcome their circumstances. Unfortunately, this isn't the case for most brothel children, as they often succumb to a life of crime, shaped by the only environment they know.

I Eat Chocolate—Arrest Me

'Arrest me, for I have consumed chocolate harvested through slave labour—I confess.'

Let me introduce Teun van de Keuken, the architect of a compelling and unconventional move to draw attention to the pervasive issue of human trafficking. A Dutch journalist, he boldly walked into an Amsterdam police station and sought arrest for the seemingly innocuous act of 'eating chocolate.' His reasoning? He believed he was complicit in supporting child slavery on cocoa farms in the Ivory Coast.

Teun's aim was clear—to secure a jail sentence, not for personal absolution, but as a means to heighten consumer awareness and compel the cocoa and chocolate industry to take decisive action against child labour. However, the legal system did not align with his plan, denying him the desired jail term.

In a thought-provoking newspaper article, Teun elucidated his rationale: 'If I am found guilty of this crime, any chocolate consumer could subsequently face prosecution. My hope is that people would cease buying chocolate, thereby denting the sales of major corporations and compelling them to address the problem.'

While I typically refrain from endorsing tactics involving public shaming for instigating change, I couldn't help but acknowledge the sound logic behind Teun's stunt. Many of us indirectly benefit from modern slavery, be it through the seafood we consume, the electronics we use, or, in some instances, the clothes we wear.

Teun's unorthodox approach garnered substantial media coverage, featuring in numerous TV, radio, and newspaper articles, effectively raising critical awareness on the issue.

Frequently, individuals approach me seeking guidance on how they can contribute to combating human trafficking. Teun's creative example serves as a testament that irrespective of one's profession, leveraging personal skills and experiences can yield innovative ways to address and alleviate the plight of those trapped in modern slavery.

As a journalist, Teun harnessed his media platform not only to report news but to make a powerful statement that resonated far beyond the confines of conventional journalism.

Three Years Undercover in Girlie Bars

'I began my journey as an undercover operative, posing as a sex buyer, when I turned twenty-four. It all started after watching a film at my church about the horrors of human trafficking. I felt a strong calling from God to take action and contribute to the fight against this heinous crime.

I joined an organization dedicated to combatting human trafficking in Pattaya, Thailand. My role involved entering bars late at night to identify underage girls. This was a challenging task as, in these establishments, women and girls would approach me, curious about my intentions. If I declined their advances and refrained from purchasing drinks, they would eventually move on. They were working girls who couldn't afford to waste time on someone who wouldn't engage with them.

When I found a girl who appeared to be under fourteen, I would try to talk to her. Many of these girls would lie about their age, but it was evident that they were younger. Sometimes, I could coax them into revealing their real age by asking about their birth date or other details.

But I had to be very careful. Long conversations without making a purchase would arouse suspicion from the pimps and madams. I was well aware of the risks involved.

The information I gathered was then shared with our NGO staff and the police, who would evaluate its validity. Sometimes, this intelligence would lead to organized raids, while other times, the authorities deemed the information insufficient.

My work was very dangerous. If anyone discovered my true intentions, I would find myself in big trouble. Many of these individuals were violent criminals, and by interfering in their illicit business, I was treading on dangerous ground. Pimps would occasionally approach me, issuing threats. They could sense that I wasn't their typical client, causing me to change locations to ensure my safety.

Despite the risks, I take immense pride in the role I played. I was able to help rescue numerous girls, although not all of them. Some proved challenging to locate, while others were unfortunately bought back by their captors. It was a constant cycle of raids and repurchasing—the grim reality of an industry driven by greed and corruption.

Given the knowledge these girls possessed about the criminal activities around them, they seldom offered any information about their pimps. It would be too dangerous for them to do so.

At times, I found myself teetering on the edge of this dark world. To blend in, I had to immerse myself in the role completely. The act became so immersive that it felt eerily real. After three years of doing this work, I decided to step away. It no longer felt like we were making a significant impact in rescuing enough victims to justify the toll it was taking on my sanity and soul. The scale of the problem was overwhelming, and we were barely scratching the surface.

It has been four years since I last set foot in one of those bars, and I doubt I will ever return. I simply cannot stomach it any more.

These days, I pray for the people of Thailand to rally and take meaningful action to assist these girls. A few isolated raids and rescues will never be sufficient. We need the government and the citizens of Thailand to care deeply about this issue. Since many of the girls hail from Myanmar and Cambodia, they often face a lack of empathy or support.'

This interview from my time in Thailand opened my eyes to the immense emotional and spiritual challenges that face those involved in undercover work within nightclubs and brothels. The toll it takes on them can be devastating.

Online Predators

'My daughter was seventeen years old when she was trafficked. She was a good girl. She seemed to enjoy school. She had good grades. But she didn't have many friends. I encouraged her to meet new people, but she wasn't sure how to do this. That is when she started to go on the computer. This is when her life began to fall apart. She met someone. Someone who had a bad heart. She was so trusting. She didn't know what was happening. I'm just glad we found out. If we hadn't, she would have been lost forever.'

Several years after moving to Hong Kong, I received a call from a woman in China who described what happened to her daughter. Her daughter felt insecure and unattractive. To find validation, she joined several online chat rooms. At first, she just simply listened and watched. Then she began to join some of the discussions.

A young man began to initiate more conversations. He described himself as a seventeen-year-old boy from Kunming, her hometown. Like her daughter, he appeared shy and reserved at first.

Over time, they began to correspond more and their online relationship grew. Whenever she had free time, she would contact her secret friend. He repeatedly told her how beautiful she was. Within two weeks, he said he had fallen in love with her.

She thought the boy was a teenager, but he was actually a middle-aged trafficker. He asked if they could meet for ice cream. When she arrived at the appointed place, the boy seen in the platform photos was there. He was part of the trafficking scheme.

In-person, he seemed less enthusiastic and much different from their chats. But she didn't care. They were in love! He picked her up from the train station and drove to a small café in the countryside.

Without knowing what happened, she woke up in a hotel room. She had been given a strong sedative that completely knocked her out for hours. The boy then revealed explicit photos of them in bed, naked. In a menacing tone, he told her that if she didn't follow his orders, he'd share the photos with her school and her family. He told her she would have to sleep with men now.

This tragic scenario happens to many young girls in China and, in fact, all over the world. While many of these girls are forced into prostitution to avoid losing face and hurting their families, in this case the girl straightaway asked her parents for help and they went to the police.

They managed to identify the 'boyfriend trafficker' and the middle-aged man who was propping him up. In this case, the girl was able to escape the trafficking trap that had been set for her. But for every girl who escapes, there are countless others who don't.

5

Modern Slavery and Me

Throughout my career combatting human trafficking, I have engaged with individuals and communities as diverse as the world is broad and wide.

Often, I have met someone whose perspective intrigued or perplexed me. Some people's viewpoints betray a lack of awareness or an oversimplification of the issue, and this only highlights the importance of education in dispelling misconceptions.

But there have been times, too, when confronted with a diversity of opinion I have been forced to re-examine my own views and adjust my own perspective.

The anecdotes below are meant to illustrate the multifaceted nature of the challenges I have faced as a frontline activist over the years.

Meena's Letter

I'm often asked what motivates me to work so hard to help address modern slavery and exploitation. Here is one example.

At a shelter in Kathmandu, I met a young woman named Meena. She had been trafficked to India and endured degrading abuse and violence at the brothel for several years. Tragically, she contracted AIDS. After several meetings, over an extended period, we became friends. Following my last visit to the shelter before leaving Nepal to work in Bangladesh, I received a powerful letter from her. It changed my life. The depth of Meena's anguish can be felt in her words. Read these words carefully—they hold a very important message.

Matthew,

Thank you for your kindness in coming to see me at the shelter. Your words brought great joy to my broken heart.

I turn fifteen on Monday. After being used by so many men, I can see that my days will soon come to an end. My illness gets worse with each passing day. I can hardly eat. The food has no flavour. It is sour, like so much of my life. I will probably not see my sixteenth birthday.

I look back on that day when I left my family's home. I was only twelve then. I was so happy. So full of life. I had such hopes and dreams. Now, look at me. I will never marry. I will never have children. I will never have grandchildren. I will not grow old.

The day that first man took my virtue was the day my God died. He and all those other men stole my life away. I was just a child. Why did nobody come to help me? I have stopped asking why this happened to me. I have even stopped feeling angry.

I need you to promise me. I need you to do what you can to prevent any other girls from falling into this hole. Promise me you will end this evil. Promise me you will never stop trying. I don't care about myself. I'm done. Don't let any more of our sisters go through what I went through.

My spirit is already dead inside. My body will soon catch up. How can this happen to a child? Where are all the good men? Where are our protectors? Where is our humanity? Promise me.

Meena

After the letter was translated for me, I read it a dozen times that day, with tears streaming down my face. Many of us who work in this field are driven by these distressing pleas. Many other victims have similar thoughts and feelings that are never revealed to the world. Meena's letter offers us a rare glimpse into their broken hearts.

There are literally millions of women and girls like Meena suffering what we cannot imagine. She asked two important questions: 'Where are all the good men (and women)? Where are our protectors?'

They are out there. We just need to find them, wake them up, and help them to work alongside us to do what we can to end this evil.

A Moral Dilemma

During the early stages of my career, I became involved in advising and supporting groups dedicated to rescuing exploited girls and women from brothels.

This typically involved receiving distressing calls about brothels harbouring underage girls who had been trafficked from Nepal. The police and NGO teams would seek my advice on the best approach, which organizations to involve, and the subsequent logistical arrangements.

Once a raid was completed, the rescued girls would be transferred to a shelter for protection and rehabilitation. However, during one such call, I was struck with horror when I discovered that they were planning to raid a brothel that had already been targeted twice before. After asking about this, I learned that despite previous raids, the authorities had been unable to permanently shut down the operation.

The brothel owner had strong connections with corrupt police officers and local officials, which allowed him to continue his illicit business despite having to surrender the girls during the previous raids. Within a week, he would procure more trafficked underage girls, and the brothel would resume its activities. It was a disheartening cycle.

It dawned on me that by solely rescuing the girls without effectively shutting down the brothel, we were inadvertently perpetuating a vicious cycle. For every ten girls rescued, ten or more would be trafficked to replace them. Our efforts were, in fact, increasing the number of victims rather than resolving the root issue.

Realizing the gravity of the situation, I called the NGO and questioned the wisdom of proceeding with the planned raid. I explained that if we continued down this path, the number of victims would only multiply. Fortunately, they agreed, and the raid was cancelled.

Though I am uncertain about the ultimate fate of that particular brothel, during my involvement in advising these operations, it remained in business. This meant that the girls recruited after we ceased the raids were not saved from this abhorrent fate. While we attempted to use our resources to pressure the government into addressing the corruption that allowed such establishments to persist, our efforts had no impact.

Throughout my career, I have been confronted with difficult, heart-wrenching choices. In this case, the solution lay in simple mathematics. Unless the brothel could be permanently shut down, conducting a raid would only contribute to the trafficking problem rather than solving it at its core.

This moral dilemma weighs heavily on my conscience even after all these years. I continue to grapple with the decision I made, forever haunted by the thought of the girls who were not saved from this nightmarish fate.

When an Act of Kindness Goes Terribly Wrong

Some time ago, I received an urgent email from an Indian businessman named Mr Gupta, who was on a work trip in Bangkok. He described a distressing incident that had occurred the previous evening before his departure back to India.

Mr Gupta explained how, during a visit to the hotel bar, a chaotic scene unfolded before him. A crazed man barged in, shouting at a young woman in Russian and forcibly dragging her towards the exit. Concerned for her well-being, Mr Gupta, along with a few other patrons, stepped forward to help. Within minutes, hotel security arrived and apprehended the man.

Filled with empathy, Mr Gupta sat down with the woman and listened to her harrowing tale. In broken English, she explained how she had fallen victim to a Russian trafficking gang that had deceived her with the promise of a hotel job in Thailand, only to force her into prostitution.

Moved by her plight, Mr Gupta made a compassionate decision. He offered to purchase a ticket for her to return to Russia and planned to accompany her partway on the journey. They would fly together to Hong Kong, after which he would return to India while she would continue her journey back home.

However, things took a turn for the worse when the woman found herself alone in her hotel room in Hong Kong. Gripped by fear, she began to have second thoughts about going back to Russia. She was terrified that the trafficking gang would track her down and harm her and her family. Her anxiety escalated, leading her to resort to excessive drinking.

In her drunken state, she reached out to Mr Gupta, who was staying in a separate hotel room, and made a distressing threat. She claimed that if he didn't stay with her, she would falsely accuse him of rape and attempted trafficking. Faced with a challenging situation, Mr Gupta tried to persuade her to return to Russia, but her behaviour became increasingly erratic. He feared that involving local authorities would result in his arrest.

Feeling desperate, Mr Gupta sought help through a mutual contact, who connected him with me. Recognizing the seriousness of the situation, I reached out to a colleague at the United Nations who stepped up and swiftly intervened. The woman received the necessary assistance from trained specialists and was safely repatriated to Russia. Mr Gupta, profoundly shaken by the experience, returned to India, having learned a valuable lesson.

While Mr Gupta's intentions were noble and rooted in compassion, he underestimated the profound trauma experienced by the trafficking victim. This scenario, unfortunately, is not uncommon. Well-meaning individuals encounter trafficking victims and feel compelled to help. But due to the intricate nature of these situations and the extreme trauma endured by the victims, it is crucial that ordinary people refrain from intervening independently. Doing so can inadvertently create further complications for both the victim and the well-intentioned individual.

Tempest in a Teapot

It was a Thursday when I participated as an observer during a raid and rescue operation at a brothel in Southeast Asia. My role involved working alongside an NGO counsellor to interview victims. Each interview was a chilling experience as I listened to the horrifying stories of what these individuals had endured—the unimaginable acts they were forced to bear, the inhumane treatment they received, the deplorable conditions they lived in, and the profound physical and emotional trauma they carried. With every interview, I felt increasingly saddened and burdened.

Among the girls we interviewed, one named Jeb stood out. She recounted her story with an astonishing lack of emotion, simply listing the facts before turning to us and asking, 'Am I free to leave? Can I go home? I need to see my mother and father. I need to find a job. I'm ready to move on.'

Considering the horrors inflicted on her, I was amazed at her calm and composed demeanour. If I had gone through what she had, I would have been completely shattered.

The following day, I boarded a flight to New York City to attend a conference. After arriving, I realized that I needed some hygiene supplies. I checked into my hotel and then stopped by a local pharmacy. I quickly grabbed the two items I needed and joined a short line at the checkout counter.

Shortly after, an argument erupted between two people ahead of me. A man accused a middle-aged woman of cutting in line and demanded that she move to the back. She ignored him and stood her ground. The situation could have been easily resolved, as there were only four of us with no more than two items each. But the man was adamant about upholding his principle of justice. He was determined to make a point.

Within moments, the heated exchange escalated into a shouting match between the two, their voices booming throughout the store. The store manager rushed over to diffuse the situation. At one point, the woman threatened to call the police, declaring that she would have the man arrested for verbal assault. This inconsequential incident had spiralled into a global crisis in their minds.

As I stood there, witnessing this 'first world problem' unfold, my thoughts drifted back to the young woman I had interviewed at the brothel just days before. She had endured being used by countless men every day for nearly two years. Her body likely bore the scars of sexually transmitted diseases and other abuse. She had suffered beatings from both customers and her ruthless pimp traffickers. Two precious years of her life had been stolen from her. She had no money, no job, and no prospects for the future. Yet, she exuded a calmness, grace, and dignity that I had seldom seen even among the envoys, heads of state, and members of royalty I had encountered in the diplomatic world.

Although part of me wanted to share this stark contrast with the people embroiled in the pharmacy dispute, I held my tongue. I realized just how vast the divide was between the two realities.

This incident reminded me of how even the most trivial concerns in the Western world can escalate and consume our attention, while far greater problems faced by countless others remain overlooked in other corners of the globe.

All I could think was that this exchange was a 'tempest in a teapot', a meaningless distraction and a waste of time for everyone involved. There are real, profound issues facing people all over the world. We all need to open our hearts and minds to them.

Am I Part of the Problem?

While working at the United Nations, I would occasionally receive emails from individuals seeking information about human trafficking. One particular exchange with an American sheds light on the inner thoughts of a man who openly admitted to engaging in sexual activities with women in the red-light districts of Thailand. The exchange, initiated by him through a referral from a friend's wife, highlights his concerns about the potential connection between his actions and sex trafficking. Here is how it went:

Sex Buyer: Dear Mr Friedman, I travel to Thailand twice a year on business. When I go, I enjoy the food, the pools, and the nightlife. I'm single. I often have fun with the girls at the bars. When I told a friend about the girls, his wife said I was supporting sex trafficking. Are the girls in the bars victims of human trafficking?

Me: Whenever you go with a person from one of those bars, you are potentially supporting human trafficking. A sizable percentage of those women are tricked and deceived into the trade. If they are under the age of eighteen, they would be considered a trafficked victim whether they choose to offer these services willingly or not.

Sex Buyer: How can they be forced if they're having fun? They all seemed so happy when I was with them.

Me: If they have been trafficked, they are often forced to bring in a quota of money each evening. If they don't, they can be beaten or abused. Knowing that a happy person is more desirable, they pretend to be having a good time. Many of the trafficking victims I have met are great actors. They have to be in order to survive.

Sex Buyer: Why don't they just run away? It's not like they are locked up. I don't believe they're held against their will.

Me: Threats can hold a person in place. Debt is also another way to control someone. Fraudulent debts are often imposed on these people with excessive interest rates. She is told she must pay it back or else. In many cases, the repayment is never tracked. They simply keep telling her she owes more and more money. They often threaten the person's family. So, locks on doors are not needed.

Sex Buyer: I've heard that these girls want to do this work. They like it. It's easier than other work.

Me: You asked me about trafficked victims. This is what my response is focused on. If a person is forced into prostitution against her will and can't leave, they fall into this category. Once again, my point is this—since you can't tell from a woman's behaviour what is motivating her to offer herself to you, she could easily be a trafficking victim.

Sex Buyer: You didn't help me with my problem. I want to keep going out with these girls. Now I don't know what to do.

Me: Based on what I said in these emails, you now know that the women in the bars in Thailand are potential sex trafficking victims. Human trafficking is illegal. What does your conscience tell you to do?

Sex Buyer: I don't know.

Some people, even when they are told what's going on, choose either to disregard that knowledge or dismiss the need for change. Unfortunately, many people, just like this man, choose to prioritize their personal gratification over changing their behaviour—even when they know it is inflicting harm on others.

Why Am I Crying?

Once, when I was onstage at a major justice conference, something unexpected happened—I began to cry. I was one of three counter trafficking experts taking part in a discussion with a well-known facilitator at the time. Near the end of our discussion, the topic turned to how we cope with the immense pain and suffering we encounter in our work.

The first response from one of the panellists was pragmatic and detached, simple and matter of fact. However, the second panellist's answer diverged from the norm. Overwhelmed by despair for the countless young victims he had observed during his time in Cambodia, he broke down in tears. Watching this grown man cry, I thought to myself, *I'm glad that is not me.*

Then the moderator directed the question to me, and a rush of memories unexpectedly flooded my mind—faces of the many helpless victims I had encountered. Suddenly, an overwhelming urge to cry engulfed me. It emanated from the depths of my gut, rising up into my eyes. With each word I spoke, the compulsion grew stronger and stronger. I couldn't contain it any longer, and I began to sob uncontrollably. The room fell silent, unsure of how to respond.

Those who had heard me speak before were accustomed to my composed and diplomatic demeanour. Yet, there I was, openly weeping for what felt like an eternity. I managed to deliver a brief statement amidst the tears. But the ordeal didn't end there. The moderator prompted the panel to address the impact of frontline work and the emotional build-up that eventually spills over. Once again, I struggled to articulate my thoughts as tears choked my words in front of a gathered audience of 150 people.

As the event was coming to an end, I felt embarrassed and wanted to immediately flee the room. But then something unexpected happened. Before I could make my escape, numerous people rushed to offer their support. Many expressed how deeply moved they were by this seminar; compassion permeated the air.

Through our shared weeping, we revealed our common humanity. The audience were touched, the message had resonated on an authentic level. That's something the most composed presentations rarely achieve.

What led to those tears? Many of us working in this field erect formidable walls to shield ourselves from the pain we encounter. These barriers serve as a defence mechanism, preventing us from feeling too much. Most of the time, they hold firm. However, there are moments when they crumble.

The moderator's question somehow pierced through my emotional fortress, exposing the unresolved pain I had been carrying. It stemmed from a deep sadness for the victims and the frustration that arises from the arduous nature of our work. Once my anguish was laid bare, I realized the need to dismantle these protective walls, allowing the healing of my own wounds. I also understood the importance of forgiving myself for not being able to help everyone—an irrational burden I had carried throughout my career, one shared by many activists.

We should never fear displaying our genuine emotions. We are all susceptible to feeling and experiencing intense emotional states. Revealing our unfiltered vulnerability is not a weakness; rather, it is a testament to our strength.

Something profound occurs when we humbly expose our true selves in the presence of others, stripped of pretence or façade.

What *Are* We Doing Wrong?

Every now and then I get a message that really baffles me. Here is one I received during the Covid pandemic:

'I read your post about using the legal system to stop human slavery. After thinking about it, I have three things to say.

You say you have been working on this topic for over thirty years. I don't understand why in this time you haven't been able to achieve more. You'd think more could be done over that time period? What are you doing wrong?

I also don't understand why this is so hard. In the UK when criminal activities take place the police take care of it. That is why we don't have any of this modern slavery in the UK. Those people in less developed countries should just pick up the phone and call the police. Have you thought about this? It seems pretty simple to me.

Are you sure there are really millions in slavery? I hear all kinds of things about global warming. But every winter it gets just as cold as the year before. I hope you and the other organizations aren't making this up to get funding. That would be pretty sad.'

I wish the fight between good and evil were so simplistic. While I often shrug these messages off, this time I was a bit frustrated. As I sat there reading and rereading this comment, I realized that I had to send something back as a rebuttal. Below is my response:

'First, I am just one person. There are an estimated 50 million victims and 500,000 traffickers. The profits generated are over $150 billion annually. Yes, I have been doing this for a long time, but what can one individual do. I wish I had the superpowers to make a significant difference—someone who could say as the result of the work I do I can help thousands and millions of people. But this is a collective action. We must all be a part of the solution.

Second, there are many trafficked persons in the UK. It isn't a 'less developed issue.' This crime can be found anywhere. Last year, less than one per cent of the criminals were convicted globally. It isn't as simple as calling the police. If it were, we wouldn't have so many people in need.

Finally, I continue to hear people question if this issue is really an issue. There are many sources of data that validate the extent of the problem. But if you start from the premise that the development sphere does this to raise money, it sounds as if you have already made up your mind. Please do some research.'

So here is the question I regularly grapple with: Why, after thirty years, are we still trying to convince people to accept this topic as real? We are talking about slavery. Millions are victims. When will the world accept how terrible and awful this crime is? What are we doing wrong?

Shelter Visit Meltdown

As a programme manager for a prominent donor agency, it was not uncommon for me to host visits from political leaders of the USA to our human trafficking programmes in the field. Given my role in managing our human rights portfolio, I often found myself guiding these officials during their visits to our project sites.

During one such congressional visit, I accompanied a distinguished US government official to a human trafficking shelter that we supported. After introducing her to the dedicated staff, the shelter's director took her on a comprehensive tour of the facility, where several girls under the age of seventeen were living. These young girls had not only been trafficked but had also been exposed to HIV/AIDS.

Curious about the experiences of the girls in the shelter, the visitor asked if anyone was willing to share their story. One courageous girl stepped forward, offering to describe her ordeal with the help of a translator. Within a mere twenty minutes of hearing the harrowing details, this middle-aged politician's composure crumbled. Initially, a few tears trickled down her cheeks, but soon she reached for a handkerchief in her bag and wept openly.

The sixteen-year-old halted her narration. She gazed at us, uncertain of how to respond to this unexpected display of vulnerability from the visitor. While I had witnessed this victim shedding tears on several occasions as she recounted her story, this was the first time she had encountered a visitor having a similar emotional reaction.

Without hesitation, the young girl approached the weeping official, took a seat beside her, and tenderly clasped her hand, offering solace. Moments later, several other girls stepped forward, offering their own gestures of support and comfort.

Throughout my career, I have encountered moments that are utterly surprising and unforeseen. Here, a group of girls who had suffered unimaginable commercial exploitation, torture, and abuse for years found themselves comforting a powerful politician. It seemed like the universe had things all backwards.

As the visitor prepared to leave, a group of girls surrounded her, held out their hands and embraced her, before she entered her vehicle.

As we drove away, the politician apologized to me for her emotional reaction. She admitted that she had been unaware of the depth and severity of the issue and was genuinely shocked by the distressing details she had learned. I assured her that her reaction was not unusual and that the revelations would be startling to anyone.

Upon returning to Washington, DC, the politician took the time to send me a heartfelt email, expressing her gratitude for the eye-opening tour. She mentioned sharing her experiences with others and assured me that she would work towards raising greater awareness and attention to this pressing issue. I'm told that she did this over several years before she retired from political life.

This story demonstrates the power of reaching people at an emotional level, not just an intellectual level. In the space of just a few minutes, this young girl had managed to influence a decision-maker in the world's most powerful capital—through little more than a heartfelt account and a human connection.

I wonder if she knew the power of her story.

Why Bother?

A few years back, I delivered a presentation on human trafficking in supply chains at a prominent business conference, during which I discussed the latest trends and emphasized the need for action.

One of the things I told the audience was, 'Last year, out of the 40 million modern slavery victims, the world only helped about

100,000, or 0.2 per cent.'[4] I also noted that this number had been consistent for several years.

Two days later, I received the following email:

'I was very intrigued to learn about your work. I didn't realize that human trafficking was such a big deal. But there was one thing that struck me. You said that an insignificant per cent of the trafficking victims gets helped. You went on to say it had been unchanged for a long time.

Here is my question. Why bother working on this topic? If all this money is spent and it has no impact, why not use it for something else? It could be fighting cancer or ending poverty or stopping world hunger.

I know this sounds brutal, but I think we need to look at the problems out there and make choices. Maybe human trafficking just can't be stopped. Maybe we just need to live with it. Maybe it is just one of those problems, like tornados. They come along and cause a bunch of damage, but you can't stop them. I hope I don't sound cold. I just think we sometimes need to be practical in our choices.'

This was not the first time I had heard this argument. In fact, it comes up at least once a year. I don't think this person was saying that he didn't care. I think he was looking at this as a failed business that was not having much impact. So, he suggested changing the business model. This is what I said in response:

'As you heard me say, the victims of human trafficking suffer unimaginable hardship. I described several cases during my presentation. As a world, we need to do whatever we can to address this kind of human rights abuse. We can never turn our back on these people in need. While the impact may not be great, we must try. This means we need to take the resources we have and do the best we can to help.

Our hope is that over time, there will be more funding, more people involved, and more impact. If more people understood the problem and took a stand, we

---

[4] Based on data from U.S. Department of State, 2024 Trafficking in Persons Report (U.S. Department of State, 2024), https://www.state.gov/reports/2024-trafficking-in-persons-report/; U.S. Department of State, 2023 Trafficking in Persons Report (U.S. Department of State, 2023), https://www.state.gov/reports/2023-trafficking-in-persons-report/

could offer more support. This would bring the numbers up. That is why I spend so much time doing presentations. I'm trying to find the people who want to help. They are out there. Are you one of them?'

I sometimes think I have a very simple mind. Having seen and felt the pain of so many trafficked people, I recognize their needs. I just don't always know how to translate this into getting others to step up and help. To me, the need to be there for our fellow men, women, and children is fundamental—self-evident even. There is no question that we must act. How can we not?

A Season of Depression

One afternoon, while working for USAID in Bangladesh, I received an email from an NGO informing me about the unfortunate passing of a fifteen-year-old trafficking victim I had known in Nepal. It was the third such notification I had received in just two months. The news was devastating. I felt utterly shattered.

During that phase of my life, I was an activist driven by anger: anger towards the criminals, anger towards the governments, anger towards the flawed system, and anger towards myself for not doing enough. The magnitude of human trafficking in the region and the grim reality that we could only assist a handful of people burdened me heavily.

Having devoted nearly a decade to anti-trafficking work, I met countless victims, witnessed the ruin inflicted upon their lives, and, gradually, their pain began to intertwine with my own. Their suffering became inseparable from my being, and I struggled to distance myself from their trauma.

Amidst such despair, I started questioning my own value in making a difference. This marked my first personal crisis. I spiralled into depression and felt defeated. Doubts crept in about the impact of my work, and I seriously thought about abandoning the cause altogether. I wondered why I shouldn't shift my focus to something less emotionally charged, something that could bring more hope and happiness into my life.

For two months, I withdrew from my commitments. I cancelled meetings, declined event invitations, and reached a point where I believed it was time to accept defeat and move on. However, one morning, as I lay in bed, a sudden realization struck me. I recognized the selfishness of my perspective. I had security, a stable job, and a promising future. Unlike those individuals whom I had fought for tirelessly, I did not face the same hardships. My personal crisis paled in comparison to the unimaginable experiences they had endured.

With this awakening, I rose from my bed and resolved to rejoin the battle. I understood that it was never about me; it was always about them—the survivors in dire need of support. My focus realigned with renewed determination.

There has always been an intrinsic drive within me, ingrained in my DNA, compelling me to tackle this issue. Since that first crash, I have experienced subsequent moments of crisis. Each time, the pattern repeats itself. I sink into deep depression, overwhelmed by the distressingly low number of people we are able to help. But somehow, my spirit rekindles, and before long, I find myself back at the drawing board, often stronger than before.

You Are a Migrant Too

One day, after one of my presentations on modern slavery, a senior banking official approached me with some questions about migration in Asia. He appeared perplexed, unable to comprehend why anyone would leave their homeland and embark on a journey filled with uncertainty and potential danger in a foreign land and culture. He admitted, 'I really can't relate to this idea. It seems so foreign to me.'

Noticing his South Asian accent, I inquired, 'Were you born here in Hong Kong?' He replied, 'No.' So, I asked him when he had come to Hong Kong, and he replied that it had been just two years ago.

Then I asked him, 'Will you be returning to your home country?' to which he answered, 'Yes, of course. My home is in India.'

So, I pointed out to him, 'You do realize that you have a lot in common with the migrants you were asking about.' Astonished, he asked, 'How so?'

Seizing the moment, I responded, 'Don't you recognize that YOU, too, are a migrant?'

A sense of realization seemed to wash over him. It appeared that he had never truly made the connection that, by definition, he, too, was a migrant.

As he stood there speechless, I probed further, asking what had brought him to Hong Kong and he replied that it was the offer of a 'great job'.

I asked if he had taken the job to improve his life and provide more opportunities for his family. He nodded.

'I hope you now understand why migrants migrate,' I said. 'Like you, they seek to enhance their lives and offer better prospects to their families. You are no different from them; you are just at a different economic level.'

I often meet people in Hong Kong who haven't fully embraced their migrant identity. Their act of 'double think' never ceases to amaze me.

As someone who has lived in four Asian countries, I, too, am a migrant. In my case, migration has brought many benefits, and I can only hope that other migrants will find their ways to similarly positive outcomes for themselves and their families.

Migration holds the potential to improve the quality of life for people from all kinds of backgrounds.

On a personal level, migration enriches our social experiences, enabling us to encounter new cultures, traditions, and languages, and fosters within us a sense of shared kinship with others.

On a societal level, the migration of skilled workers drives economic growth.

Our sole mission, when it comes to migration, should be to ensure that every outcome is safe and positive for the person involved.

Why Do Grown-Ups Let Modern Slavery Exist?

Several years ago, I gave a presentation on modern slavery to a fifth-grade class. Knowing their age, I focused on forced labour, without delving into the topic of sex trafficking. I shared with them that out of the staggering 50 million victims, the world had managed to help only 115,000, which was less than one half per cent.[5] I explained that this was due to the immense profits involved and the unfortunate lack of people dedicated to fighting this problem. When I finished, I opened the floor for questions, and the eager students raised their hands in anticipation.

The initial questions were straightforward, but then one student caught my attention with a perplexed expression on his face. 'You told us that slavery is one of the worst crimes a person can do, something that causes a lot of harm to other people,' he said. 'So why doesn't the world come together to stop the bad guys from doing this?'

All the students leaned forward, waiting for my response.

Feeling the weight of their earnest curiosity, I replied, 'It is a complex thing.' I rattled off some standard responses and general explanations and noted some of the many challenges my work involves. But even in my own head, I realized I was stumbling to find a satisfactory answer. The perplexed expression on the student's face remained.

He continued, 'I don't understand. If something is so terrible, how can it still happen? Why aren't people talking about it? Why aren't there armies fighting against it? Why aren't our parents joining the fight?'

I was stumped. The truth was, I had asked myself the same questions countless times. Admitting my lack of an answer, I found myself in agreement with these young minds. The world continues to help only 0.2 per cent of the victims, and this number remains the same year after year.[6] Why?

---

[5] Ibid.

[6] Ibid.

At that moment, the teacher intervened and attempted to rephrase my explanations. Sensing the urgency in the room, he moved the discussion forward, asking if anyone else had a question.

A girl sitting in the back raised her hand and boldly asked, 'Why don't you adults fix this? I still don't understand. Why can't you answer this question?'

The astuteness of these students struck a chord within me. They were right. We should all be asking this question. It is a question that should be on the lips of governments, corporations, the United Nations, faith-based groups, schools, and society at large. We must not shy away from it, but confront it head on. The fact that so few victims are being helped each year is a glaring injustice that demands urgent attention and action.

In their innocence and clarity, these young students had got to the heart of the issue.

Unsatisfactory Speech

A few years ago, I was in Australia doing a fundraiser for a small NGO that was offering vocational training and employment for sex trafficking victims. The venue was small but very comfortable. Nearly thirty people attended the event.

I did a short twenty-minute presentation related to the importance of this topic and offered a shout-out to the sponsoring organization. This included a few stories related to my own experiences and a short description of what can be done by each of us to help address the issue. I was happy with the outcome.

After the talk, a person came up to me in a very aggressive manner. With his finger pointed inches from my face, he repeatedly insisted that there were things that I should have mentioned but I didn't. He went on and on about how I failed to convey priority points.

I tried to explain that in a twenty-minute presentation, a presenter has limited time and content choices must be made. I also explained that I tried to convey a message that would inform and inspire. But he didn't listen to any of this.

Now and then I face situations like this. As public speakers, we must decide what content is right for the audience. While I don't always get this right, I never could understand those who come up and criticize what is being said by someone who is just trying to help.

Here are two other emails I received from people who said similar things at different times:

'Your presentation should have included more details about government corruption. This is the real issue. By not stating this, you failed to convey anything meaningful to the audience. I walked away feeling very disappointed. Don't you know anything about this topic?'

'Unsatisfactory. That is all I have to say. Unsatisfactory. As I said in my comment to you, you need to work with the police. If only people like you would take my advice, we could stop this problem. The police are there to serve. If you call them up, they will arrest the criminals. I don't know why you don't see this. You don't seem to understand anything.'

In this second case, I tried to explain to this person from Canada that in some locations, corruption exists among police departments. He simply couldn't get his head around this idea.

Moving from NGOs to the Private Sector

When I transitioned from traditional humanitarian work within the public sector, which involved collaborating with governments, NGOs, and the United Nations, to working with corporations and banks as the CEO of The Mekong Club, I had to make many adjustments. I quickly noticed striking differences in working styles, approaches, and expectations within the fast-paced private sector. This disparity became evident during a crucial donor meeting I had in Hong Kong early on in my new role.

Through a mutual connection, I was invited to give a presentation to three influential industry leaders. Armed with my eighty-seven-slide PowerPoint deck, I began my talk. However, to my surprise, after only a few slides, one of them interrupted and asked, 'Are you almost done?' Caught off guard, I felt flustered and rushed through my presentation.

Another executive inquired, 'Tell me what is broken and what is needed to fix it.' And yet another challenged me, saying, 'I'm giving you this one chance to convince me. So, convince me.'

In the private sector, there is an expectation that the presenter knows their subject matter and can succinctly summarize the problem at hand, along with proposed solutions. They value a concise approach that focuses on identifying what is not working and outlining the necessary steps to fix it.

Unfortunately, my typical NGO approach, which involved comprehensive presentations, was neither appreciated nor well-received. I left the meeting empty-handed, but the experience served as a valuable lesson, prompting me to reassess and adapt my strategies.

In the NGO world, we often deliver detailed programme pitches, carefully guiding our audience through a series of assumptions, rationales, objectives, and activities. To address all potential concerns, we strive to cover every aspect of our proposal in great detail, supported by relevant data. Content is regarded as crucial.

My personal presentation style also hindered my transition. For nearly ten years, I had made a habit of wearing Ralph Lauren–style polo shirts as my work attire. When I was with the United Nations, my shirt featured the UN emblem, and when I joined The Mekong Club, I wore shirts with our organization's logo. Even after shifting to the private sector, I continued wearing these casual shirts to all my events for the first three years.

Despite my staff's suggestions that I wear a button-down shirt with a tie, I resisted, feeling that it contradicted my identity. I had an independent streak and was determined to stay true to myself.

However, I soon discovered that my choice of attire was causing misunderstandings and hindering my ability to connect with corporate leaders. Often, when I arrived at conferences in my polo shirt to deliver a keynote speech, I was mistaken for a delivery person or a venue manager. I found myself waiting on the sidelines, appearing out of place amidst the sea of impeccably dressed individuals. It was only after my speech that people realized who I was and why I was there.

It took several instances where executives mistook me for someone else to realize that my wardrobe was not conducive to winning over corporations and encouraging their participation in our association—a community of professionals dedicated to eradicating modern slavery.

One day, I had an epiphany. I decided to wear a shirt and tie, and from that moment on, things quickly changed. I came to understand that adapting to the unspoken norms and expectations of different communities was necessary to make a lasting impact. Wearing a tie didn't alter my identity; it simply removed distractions and enhanced my potential to effectively deliver my message.

Americans Don't Care What Happens to People in Asia

Below is an email exchange I had with an American friend of the family. It provides a glimpse into an all-too-common perspective.

'Dear Matt,

I read some of the human trafficking articles you wrote. You told me to be honest, so let me be honest. I didn't like them much. I don't know why you keep focusing on such depressing topics. After reading this, I felt so sad. Why do you always have to write about subjects that are hard to read? I will never understand this about you.

As an American, I don't think these articles would have any appeal. Americans don't like reading about people in other countries. We want to read about people in our own country. What difference does it make to us if these things happen? That is their reality, not ours. I just can't relate. We all know that there are poor people out there who experience bad things. That is just the way the world is.

I don't know how this happened, but you seem to obsess over these poor, disenfranchised people. Maybe you have been overseas too long. Why can't you just write about the good things in life? Why can't you write about things that are happy? I know you don't want to hear this, but people just don't care about what happens to people in Asia.

*Regards,
Susan.'*

Here is my response:

'Dear Susan,

Thanks for reading my articles. I asked you to be honest, and as always, you were very clear with your response. You have reflected the views of many. But despite your critique, I plan to continue writing these stories. Not because I hope to influence Americans, but because I think these are stories that need to be told.

Each day, thousands of young people throughout the world experience all kinds of hardships—poverty, discrimination, sexual abuse, hunger, disease, and more. These are real stories that are unfolding with real people. To me, it doesn't matter if a person comes from India or New York. A person is a person is a person. The fact that many people out there don't think this is relevant to their life is precisely why I think such stories need to be shared. What happens to a girl in India should be just as important to us all as what happens to a person in New York or anywhere else.

Yes, the material is not happy, it is sad and depressing. But if it is hard for us to read this, then imagine how hard it is for others to actually experience it.

I appreciate your honesty and your insights. In some ways, you have encouraged me to spend even more time with these articles.

*Warm regards,
Matt.'*

I face these kinds of opinions all the time. I know many Americans and others from the West who do care about the world. So, I don't accept this generalization.

What's the Store's Policy on Slavery?

After delivering a talk on modern slavery at a public library in Hartford, Connecticut, I was approached by a group of ten university students who were eager to help. They wanted a simple project that they could do as a group. Seizing the opportunity, I proposed a field experiment and they readily agreed.

I began by asking whether their hometown had a prominent department store, to which they responded 'Yes'.

So I suggested to them: 'Every day, at the same time, one of you can visit the store and politely ask to speak with the manager. Pose the question, 'How do you ensure that the items in this store are not connected to human trafficking?'

I emphasized the importance of maintaining a non-threatening approach and encouraged them to explain their student group's dedication to combating human trafficking over the next ten days if prompted by the manager. I also asked them to keep me updated on their progress.

Here's what they reported: 'During the initial three days, the manager responded consistently, saying, 'I don't know.' On the fourth day, he had a piece of paper containing his company's policy in hand. By the fifth day, he could articulate the policy's basic elements without needing the document. On the seventh day, he proudly displayed the policy on a bulletin board near the store's entrance. Finally, on the tenth day, copies of the policy were available near the checkout counters.'

According to the students, the store manager displayed genuine interest in the topic, asking numerous questions about their project and its significance. Despite the repetitive nature of their inquiries, he remained supportive and receptive. Not all managers would react positively to such persistence, but this particular one embraced the opportunity.

These small actions can effectively communicate to companies that the public cares deeply about the issue of human trafficking. I have often found that companies respond supportively when approached in a positive manner. It's a powerful catalyst for driving change.

But Trafficking Keeps My iPhone Cheap . . .

During one of my presentations at a local high school, I delved into the harrowing realities of modern slavery, emphasizing the horrific conditions its victims must labour under. I concluded by urging the audience to use their purchasing power as consumers to combat this issue.

Following the talk, I took a few questions from the students before making my way out. Just as I was about to leave, a sixteen-year-old student approached me. She expressed regret that there wasn't enough time to ask her question during the session. Then, with a hesitant tone, she said, 'I'm just a high school student with limited money. If we solve the trafficking problem, won't products like iPhones become more expensive? It would then be difficult for me to afford the things I want. Isn't that also a problem, especially for students like me?'

I paused, unsure if I had correctly grasped her concern. Eventually, I asked, 'Are you suggesting that we should avoid addressing the issue of modern slavery to keep smartphone prices low for students?' She didn't respond verbally, but her eyes indicated she awaited my reply.

In response, I said, 'Throughout my presentation, I described the immense pain and suffering endured by those subjected to forced labour. Nobody should have to endure such inhumane treatment. It is our collective responsibility to contribute towards their liberation. If that means paying a bit more for certain products, don't you think it's a reasonable trade-off to prevent such atrocities?'

She tilted her head slightly and replied, 'I suppose so. I just worry about my ability to afford things I want.'

I remember walking away, thinking to myself, *I'm glad that she didn't ask that question in front of her peers. They would have found it as shocking as I did.*

Months later, during another talk, that very same question was asked by a student in front of the entire audience. I held my breath, anticipating a backlash from the others. Yet, to my astonishment, many leaned forward, eager to hear my response. No outrage after all.

I was utterly taken aback. Their reaction left me in a state of disbelief. In fact, I'm still grappling with their response. Could this be the reason why there are so few consumer boycotts against products associated with human trafficking? Would consumers genuinely prioritize lower prices over eradicating modern slavery? If so, their indifference chills me to the bone.

Based on this experience, I fear that certain fundamental ethical and moral foundations within society require some kind of restoration. If students prioritize their personal desire for affordable items over someone else's most basic human rights, then we have a lot of work ahead of us.

Sheltered Housewives

During my time in Nepal, I met a group of compassionate housewives who had been deeply moved by some articles they had read about the sex trafficking of Nepalese girls. Courageously, they had decided to lend a helping hand. They pooled their money and rented a shelter to provide a safe haven for those affected. Their noble aim was not only to provide food and shelter to five trafficked girls, but to empower them through job training and healthcare too.

On the day of the shelter's launch, I arrived to an awe-inspiring sight. The shelter was a haven of comfort and care. Immaculate beds, adorned with freshly folded sheets and soft pillows, stood in neat alignment. The walls, painted with care and love, exuded a sense of serenity. At the foot of each bed stood a wooden locker containing a collection of stuffed animals.

From the moment I stepped inside, it was evident that these women had envisioned a heart-warming welcome for the girls who would seek refuge here. They imagined five young girls stepping out of the van, their eyes filled with relief and hope. Overwhelmed with joy, tears of happiness would well up as they glimpsed their beautifully prepared rooms. The stuffed animals would be tenderly lifted from the beds, hugged, and cherished.

As we waited for them to arrive, I asked a few questions about the girls' backgrounds. I was told that most were sixteen years old and had been in the Mumbai brothels for many years. After hearing this, I wondered if their storybook meeting would happen as envisioned.

When the van pulled up, the air was full of anticipation. But within seconds of the girls stepping out the mood changed. Instead of five young, submissive girls expecting a welcome hug, they turned out to be teenagers dressed in revealing outfits. From the moment they arrived, their facial expressions revealed their disdain.

When the welcoming committee walked up to them, both sides stopped, not knowing what to do. After a short, awkward speech, the girls were escorted into the shelter.

One girl jumped onto the first bed she saw, pushing the stuffed animals onto the floor. An argument broke out over who should get the bed closest to the windows. Two of the girls faced off—shouting, pushing, and using foul language.

No one had prepared the sheltered housewives for this potential outcome. Brothel life is filled with drugs, alcohol, swearing, fighting, surviving—and things far, far worse. Living and working in one for years on end completely changes a person.

After walking into the sewing room, one of the ladies explained that each girl would be taught how to sew.

One girl laughed out loud and said, 'They expect me to learn to use that thing? Are they kidding? They want me to sit and sew for ten hours a day—no way. I can go outside and spread my legs and get a full day's wage in fifteen minutes.' The room fell silent.

While I never revisited the shelter, I learned things went from bad to much worse. As days turned into weeks, the girls grew increasingly defiant and unruly. And then, one day, everything changed. Without warning, the girls simply wandered off, one by one. With the departure of the last girl, the shelter's doors closed, never to reopen.

This sobering experience shows the importance of understanding the realities of the world we inhabit, and reminds us that it may not always align with our expectations, however well-intentioned.

Video Killed the Romeo Pimp

The trafficking of young girls from Myanmar to Thailand for the purpose of sexual exploitation often involves the manipulative tactics of 'lover boys' or 'Romeo pimps' who act as recruiters. These traffickers target vulnerable girls who come from families facing challenges such as alcoholism, gambling, abuse, extreme poverty, debt, or neglect.

The trafficker, a teenage boy around her age, begins by befriending the girl, displaying kindness, sweetness, and patience. Through affectionate gestures and small gifts, he carefully builds a sense of trust, making the girl believe he genuinely cares for her. As their bond grows, they spend more time together, deepening her attachment to him.

Eventually, the trafficker suggests a day trip to the Thailand border, taking advantage of its porous nature in certain areas. The plan is to cross over, go shopping and dining, and return home unnoticed. Since such an excursion would be disapproved of by most parents, the 'boyfriend' convinces the girl to lie, claiming she will be spending the day with her girlfriends.

What is his real plan? They will embark on a six-hour bus journey to the border, cross it, and then the girl will be either drugged or swiftly abducted by waiting accomplices in a van. This sudden act separates her from everything familiar and thrusts her into the harrowing world of trafficking.

But one non-governmental organization (NGO) came up with a clever plan to tackle this ruse. Noting that buses along the border often play movies to entertain passengers, it created a fifteen-minute film that vividly depicted the entire process of 'Romeo trafficker' recruitment and asked the buses to play this in between programmes.

Imagine a girl, unknowingly seated next to her own trafficker, realizing that scenes from her own life are playing out on screen. The video depicts each stage of the 'Romeo's' ruse—from the initial contact and affectionate grooming to the romantic trip across the border, and the horrifying moment of drugging and trafficking.

This powerful film helped many girls to realize the imminent danger they were in, allowing them to save themselves. Many would get off the bus immediately and seek help from border guards or the police.

I deeply admired this NGO for its novel idea. It has saved many girls from the clutches of slavery and a lifetime of indescribable suffering.

A CEO Sees the Light

During my final year working for the United Nations in Bangkok, I made a series of trips to Hong Kong to engage with business leaders about modern slavery. With a staggering 82 per cent of trafficking victims connected to private sector supply chains, I was eager to hear the perspectives of these influential individuals.

Arranging these meetings through my project assistant, we would secure appointments months in advance. The United Nations had a way of opening doors. However, upon reaching the offices, I occasionally encountered a distinct change in the atmosphere. Some business leaders seemed distressed, almost as if they had forgotten about our scheduled meeting.

I recall overhearing one person mutter, 'I completely forgot about this. I don't even know why I agreed to it. Well, might as well get it over with.' In this particular instance, the individual I met with initially declared that he had only fifteen minutes to spare, insisting he had pressing work and continued typing emails on his iPhone.

Nevertheless, within ten minutes, a transformation had occurred. As I began my presentation, sharing some of my most poignant stories about human trafficking, his attention shifted from the screen to me. Gradually, he set aside his phone and became fully engaged in the conversation. Despite his earlier time constraints, our discussion lasted nearly 90 minutes.

This was not an isolated incident—similar encounters have occurred repeatedly throughout my career and usually follow a common pattern. First, it becomes apparent that a business leader has limited exposure to the extent and gravity of the trafficking issue. Consequently, when they are confronted with the stark reality, they become open to learning more. Then, as they begin to comprehend the extent of the problem and recognize its relevance to their own business operations, their curiosity grows, prompting them to ask insightful questions.

Over the years, I have realized that many individuals remain uninformed about the darkest corners of our world. But when people are confronted with the harsh reality, it usually captures their attention and stirs their emotions.

In the case of the businessman with supposedly only 15 minutes to spare, an astonishing transformation occurred. Over time, he became an ardent champion for the cause. The issue resonated deeply with him and eradicating it from his industry became his personal mission. A year after my initial discussion with him, he became a do-gooder junkie. I could hardly keep up with him. In fact, this was his testimony to me:

'I really feel good about myself. I now realize I can do my day job and help the world on the side as a volunteer. That void—that persistent feeling that something important was missing in my life—is now gone. I have a purpose. My kids think it is so cool that I am helping to end modern slavery. I don't know why it took me so long to do this. I wish I had started much earlier.'

Engaging in acts of service and helping others brings immense personal satisfaction. It is impossible not to experience a profound sense of fulfilment when one contributes to a cause that makes a positive impact on the lives of others, particularly one as critical as modern slavery.

A Chance Encounter on the Train to Toronto

After a 4.5-hour flight from Vancouver to Toronto, I swiftly collected my bag and caught the city train just as it was about to depart. Breathing heavily, I plopped into a seat, feeling relieved.

Beside me sat an elderly African American woman, who noticed my breathlessness and kindly placed a hand on my arm. 'Slow down,' she said gently. 'There's no need to rush. You have all the time in the world.' Her words resonated with me, and I smiled, taking her advice to heart.

As I settled into my seat and opened my laptop, the woman glanced over and asked, 'Are you doing a presentation on slavery?' Surprised by her observation, I nodded and replied, 'Yes, I am. I'm currently on a presentation tour across North America, addressing this subject.'

With a gentle smile, she asked, 'What do you know about slavery?' I proceeded to explain that I had dedicated over thirty years to working on the issue. I shared some case examples, described the nature of the problem, and discussed the staggering numbers and prevailing trends.

Bewildered, she confided, 'I don't understand. How can slavery still exist today? With all the police and laws we have in place, how can people find themselves in such a situation? It simply doesn't make any sense to me. My own family endured slavery for a long time, and they were freed many years ago. I thought we had left it all behind.'

Sympathetically, I responded, 'Modern slavery may differ from traditional slavery, but the outcome remains the same. People lose control over their freedom, decision-making, and ability to make choices. They are trapped by debt and threats.'

For a while, she remained silent, her expression reflecting her confusion. Eventually, she turned to me and asked, 'What needs to be done to fix this issue?'

I explained, 'We need to raise awareness. We must encourage individuals to step up and take a stand. It's crucial to inspire empathy and ignite concern for the 50 million men, women, and children trapped in these dire circumstances.'

Curiously, she inquired further, 'Martin Luther King delivered a speech about being free at last, free at last. Do you give speeches like that in your presentations?' With a smile, I replied, 'I deliver over 180 presentations a year, but my speeches are not quite like his. His was a historic, life-changing address that impacted countless lives.'

Contemplating my words, she looked at me earnestly and suggested, 'You should craft your own 'free at last' speech. That's what's needed to mobilize people to lend a hand. They need to be inspired in that manner. Now that I'm aware of this issue, I'll speak to my church and see what can be done. Although I came to Toronto to attend a film festival with my sister, perhaps my true purpose for being in Canada was for you to sit beside me and enlighten me about this terrible matter. God works in mysterious ways.'

As the train arrived at Union Station, I handed her my business card, and she expressed her intention to contact me. Although I never heard from her again, I sensed that this chance encounter would ignite her determination to take action. I could see it in her eyes.

Life often surprises us with serendipitous moments when we seek something else, only to realize that what we find is more aligned with our needs than what we initially pursued. That's precisely what unfolded with this chance encounter with this woman.

These Are the Countries with no Human Trafficking

Every year, I have the privilege of delivering about thirty presentations to students across Asia. I am particularly enthusiastic about engaging with young people because of their natural curiosity and their fervent desire to make a positive impact on the world. Over time, many of these students have remained in contact with me, some since their middle school days, seeking career advice in the humanitarian and human rights sectors. I am proud to say that a few of them have even embarked on anti-trafficking roles.

During my presentation on global modern slavery, I employ a thought-provoking technique. I tell the students that I am going to reveal a list of countries with no human trafficking, and I ask them to share their guesses of which countries will be on this list. They eagerly respond with answers such as Norway, Sweden, the USA, Canada, and Japan—mostly countries from the Western world.

Once their responses have exhausted, I display a slide featuring an empty table. I then proceed to say, 'Trafficking exists everywhere. There are virtually no countries in the world that do not face this problem.' I go on to describe how this issue unfolds across different regions through deception, coercion, and the exploitation of vulnerable individuals.

I began including this anecdote in my presentation after a prominent Asian banking professional wrote me the following message:

'As you know, Matt, I come from Asia where slave trafficking and sex trafficking are unfortunately very common, and the police turn a blind eye because they are paid off by the traffickers.

But trafficking is also present in the US and developed countries, where it could start as a romance scam, or as an enticement of modelling and other job opportunities, drugs, etcetera. Please also talk about this to create awareness, otherwise your presentations make it appear to be an Asia problem in poorer developing countries. The message should be that it can happen to anyone anywhere. If you stand outside Port Authority Bus Station in Manhattan, you don't need to be an expert to see young women being trafficked despite the heavy presence of police.'

Her message resonated deeply with me. Trafficking and exploitation of individuals do indeed occur globally. I realized that to truly engage my audiences, I needed to provide local examples that would help people to recognize trafficking is a problem in their own community.

The message I need to get across is this can happen to anyone, anywhere.

Humbug, Humbug, Humbug

Years ago, I delivered a keynote speech at a hotel in Singapore for a marketing company, focusing on modern slavery and its connection to the private sector. However, the event took an unexpected turn when I was heckled throughout my entire talk by an older British man who repeatedly exclaimed 'humbug' at regular intervals. Despite pausing in the hope that someone would address his aggressive behaviour, no one in the audience responded.

When the question-and-answer session finally arrived, the man wasted no time in sharing his views: 'You do-gooder types are always fabricating stories about non-existent problems. There are no slaves today. This is all complete nonsense.'

In response, I calmly stated, 'These statistics do not come from me; they come from reputable research institutions and the United Nations. And based on my own personal experience of interviewing countless victims, I can assure you that modern slavery is a very real issue.'

The man laughed dismissively and retorted, 'United Nations? What a joke! And I'm sure you've spoken to some workers who were simply cheated by their employers, or some unhappy individuals involved in the sex trade,' he sneered. 'These people are not slaves. They are merely discontented individuals concocting stories to evoke sympathy. You NGO-types fall for it every time. I have been conducting business here in Asia for thirty years, and I have never once encountered a single slave. Humbug.'

As his rant continued without a break, one of the event organizers finally intervened. Frustrated that he couldn't freely express his opinion, the man stood up and marched out of the room.

Half an hour later, I spotted him in the lobby talking with a group of people. Sensing an opportunity to further defend my position, I took a seat, wrote down several website names and document titles, and approached him. My request that he consider reading through the materials was initially met with refusal. But after I persisted in a kind, patient manner, he reluctantly agreed. Two weeks later, I received a heartfelt apology from him, acknowledging that he had been mistaken in his beliefs.

Despite his initially aggressive approach, I never took offense. This wasn't the first time someone had expressed disbelief regarding the topic of modern slavery. Allow me to share two other statements I received:

'I am thirty-four years old, and I am finding out about this terrible thing just now? I don't understand why this isn't front-page news. Are you sure this topic is for real?'

'I sat there and listened in disbelief. I just couldn't get my head around the concept of slavery. I still don't know whether I believe it or not.'

When confronted with the topic of modern slavery for the first time, its shocking nature often leaves people incredulous. However, it should not remain this way. We must find effective methods to educate people across all levels of society—businesses, schools, clubs, religious organizations, and the general public. This education should be ongoing and consistent.

Blaming these individuals would be unfair, as they simply lack awareness. The subject matter we are discussing is entirely new to them. We, the counter-trafficking community, must do better in our efforts to inform people. If individuals are unaware of an issue, they will not feel compelled to care. And without care, there can be no action.

What it Takes to End this Madness

I often encounter the word 'no'. Countless people have told me, 'There's no way we can tackle the issue of human trafficking. It's too massive.'

Following a presentation at an NGO office, a Catholic deacon said something very disheartening to me. He said, 'Stop believing you can put an end to this. Slavery is like a cancer. It's incurable and unfixable. Your hopeful, inspirational words are meaningless. They offer only empty promises. Accept this reality. It's impossible to stop. Impossible.'

In response to his pessimism, I presented a hypothetical scenario. I asked him to consider a massive asteroid hurtling towards Earth. Let's imagine that the only way to prevent it from impacting our planet was to eradicate modern slavery within the next two years. Could humanity achieve such a feat?

'Absolutely,' I said. 'What might initially seem impossible would become a formidable challenge. We would explore and utilize every resource at our disposal. Considering the remarkable ingenuity of humankind, I firmly believe we could find a viable solution. Saving our Earth and its inhabitants would serve as an incredibly compelling motivation. So yes, theoretically, it could be possible.'

He remained silent. I had made my point. My intention was clear: Where there is a will, there is a way. Without a compelling motivation to end it, modern slavery will persist with impunity.

What is required to bring about this change? Nothing less than the collective effort of every one of us. It is time to move beyond mere thoughts and take action. Each of us must take a stand. That includes you, dear reader. I hope you've been shocked by what you've read in these chapters, shocked enough to want to do something about it, to join the fight even in some small way.

The good news is that it is within the power of every one of us to help. Changing the world starts with a simple step. To be part of the solution, try vocalizing and staying true to the following statement:

> 'I have learned about the 50 million people trapped in forced prostitution and labour, and I condemn this crime against humanity. I pledge to educate myself about this issue and spread awareness to others. I will share this message within my family, workplace, and community, and dedicate myself to

help in any way I can. I will be a voice for the many who are suffering and desperate and trapped as modern-day slaves.'

It might seem impossible that one person could make a dent against an evil as pervasive as this, yet if we all unite with this objective, we can help countless individuals. To get there we must first open our hearts to the injustices of our world. In the beginning, there must be empathy.

Part Two

Awakening

'We are shaped by our experiences, both positive and negative, which define us at any given point in our lives. Like a flowing river, these experiences continuously influence and mould us, shaping the person we are and the person we become. Each day brings new experiences that reshape us, making us different from who we were yesterday and who we will be tomorrow.'

—BJ Neblett, author, and instructor
at Seattle's famed Hugo House for Writers

How Did I Get to Where I Am?

Reflecting on my life's journey, I've come to recognize that my path towards becoming an international activist fighting modern slavery had its roots in my earliest years. Somehow my upbringing had steered me towards a human rights career spanning four decades.

My first exposure to human trafficking occurred in 1991 when I was thirty, working on HIV programmes for USAID in Nepal. During this time, I encountered numerous women and girls forced into prostitution and this had a profound impact on me, motivating me to become a frontline advocate. Subsequent tours in Bangladesh,

Thailand, and Hong Kong deepened my understanding and experience in the field.

However, the seeds of my journey were planted much earlier, in my youth, during my formative years as a shy boy from a small New England town. The transformation from that reserved young man into a global activist didn't follow the typical trajectory of driven teenage activists. My early aspirations were centred around making money, leading a comfortable life, and pursuing personal happiness.

So, what triggered my transition? What compelled me to stand up for justice across more than forty countries? What forces guided me in this direction, turning it into my life's mission?

To answer these questions, I embarked on an introspective journey through time. This exploration revealed the unexpected twists and turns from the earliest years of my life that had influenced, changed, and defined me.

I realized that seemingly insignificant moments had in fact played great parts in shaping my destiny.

There was no direct line, no one thing, connecting all these experiences. Rather, my journey was shaped by a myriad of milestones, successes, and failures—some interconnected, others not—that brought me to where I am today.

A mentor once told me, 'In the past forty-five years, you've probably had only 200 to 300 truly memorable days. There was something about them that stood out. They were significant and meaningful. You may not know why. They just were.'

I've come to realize that these benchmark memories define us, shedding light on our thoughts, emotions, and actions, and guiding us through life. They elucidate the paths we take, the choices we make, and how we arrived at our present state.

Part Two of this book is my attempt to identify these memories and weave them together to make sense of my journey. This is done through the collection of short stories that reflect events and circumstances in my life that influenced who I am today.

Before we dive into these memories, I would like to leave you with one last thought. I did not consciously choose this path; in many ways, it chose me. It consumed me entirely, leaving no room for a different course.

Although some may commend my actions over the years as heroic, I cannot claim deliberate intent behind them. I must confess, I acted because I could not do otherwise.

Many times, I yearned to turn away, to release myself from the torment. Life would have been easier, less burdened. But I could not, as I had never voluntarily offered my services in the first place; they were demanded of me by an inscrutable force that I have never fully comprehended or controlled.

At the same time, engaging in this work has not detracted from my existence; on the contrary, it has enriched and added value to it.

My battle against human trafficking continues, and my unwavering commitment persists. While the path I have trodden has been strewn with pain and hardship, it has also been illuminated by the resilient spirits of survivors and the knowledge that even the smallest efforts can make a difference.

6

Coming of Age: My Earliest Memories

Childhood is the canvas upon which we paint the tapestry of our future lives. It is the star that guides us as we navigate the complexities of adulthood and fuels our determination to make a difference in the world. The anecdotes that follow are some of my most memorable and precious childhood experiences. It's within these short stories that I have finally found myself, that I have come to understand how I got to where I am.

My Family Left Me Alone on the Beach

When I was a little kid, my parents would take us on day trips to Rocky Neck beach along the Connecticut shore every summer. It was a cherished tradition for me and my five siblings. On one particular hot summer day in July, we arrived early in the morning and spent five blissful hours basking in the sun, playing in the sand, swimming, exploring the jetty for crabs, and enjoying a nourishing lunch. For a five-year-old boy like me, it was paradise.

When it was finally time to leave, my mother supervised us as we all gathered our belongings, including blankets, beach umbrellas, coolers, and clothes. This process was always a bit disorganized and chaotic, but on this particular day it was especially so. As our motley crew made its way to the parking lot on the other side of the train tracks, something unfortunate happened—my parents, unintentionally, left me there by myself. How did this happen?

While I was lost in my own little world, I became distracted and wandered off towards the ocean.

When I returned to our spot, to my dismay, they were all gone. Fear gripped me and panic overwhelmed me. I felt light-headed and my world began to spin. Tears welled in my eyes, and I began to cry, questioning why they had abandoned me.

Thankfully, the lifeguard noticed my distress and rushed to help. A small crowd of bystanders, including parents and kids, gathered as I struggled to explain that I had been left behind. I choked on my words and was unable to overcome my sobs.

Interestingly, my recollection of these events differed greatly from my mother's. In my mind, hours had passed before my family returned, while my mother insisted it was only about ten minutes. In my portrayal of the story, I was a brave child who had shed only a few tears, whereas my mother remembers me bawling uncontrollably like a helpless baby.

While I was convinced that they had left me behind on purpose, my mom's take was that with six kids, sometimes things like this happen. It wasn't a big deal.

Whatever the truth of the matter, I am grateful this story had a happy ending. My family did eventually find me, and we went home together. It became my first unforgettable memory.

So why does this incident stand out among the many early memories I have? Perhaps it is because, for the first time in my life, I felt truly alone. My family seemed to vanish into thin air, and I found myself lost without a way back home. The memory of that feeling lingers within me to this day.

Since then, I have been in many situations that triggered in me a similar sense of abandonment. Even now, I often wonder if that day on the beach had a far greater impact on me than I initially realized.

Grandma's Close Call

When I was a young boy, my first encounter with human trafficking demonstrated to me that this evil world was capable of impacting any family, including my own.

That first encounter came through a story my mother told me about Dora, a young and attractive twenty-three-year-old woman who had embarked on a journey from Germany to reunite with her husband in Los Angeles, California.

The couple were new immigrants to the USA; Dora's husband had travelled ahead to find a place to live and a job to support their new life. After a long and solitary boat trip, Dora found herself in New York City, where she boarded a train bound for California.

Upon arriving in Chicago, the halfway point, she mistakenly believed that she had arrived in Los Angeles. Desperate for confirmation, she questioned those around her, but she spoke only German and couldn't find anyone on the train platform who understood her.

At that moment, fate appeared to intervene. A young man fluent in German noticed her distress and offered to help, claiming that he had been sent by Dora's husband to accompany her to their new home in California, which he said was nearby.

Unbeknownst to Dora, this man was a white slaver—a trafficker who exploited vulnerable women and girls for profit. He intended to take her off to one of the seedy brothels on the outskirts of the city. Once trapped in this unforgiving hellhole, she would have been lost forever.

Fortunately, however, just as she was about to leave with this stranger, a German couple recognized the danger unfolding before them. Acting swiftly, they rescued Dora from his clutches and ensured her safe return to the train.

Dora was my grandmother. My mother shared this harrowing incident with me when I was just five years old.

You see, at that age, I tended to regularly wander off alone to places unsuitable for a young child, including a nearby forest called Cedar Mountain. My mother discovered this after finding a collection of lava rocks hidden beneath a bush outside our house. The only place these rocks were found was in the forest along the trails on this mountain. When she asked me where they came from, I lied. I said I didn't know how they got there. Sensing my deception, she decided to teach me a crucial lesson about the existence of evil individuals in the world through my grandmother's dramatic story.

From the first time I heard this tale, I grasped the sobering truth that deceitful people roam the earth, preying on others and snatching away their freedom. This realization thoroughly frightened me, as even at such a tender age I understood that had my grandmother fallen into the clutches of the white slaver, I might never have come into existence.

The memory of my grandma's close call remained with me throughout the years. It served as my introduction to the existence of malevolence in the world and instilled in me a cautious approach to strangers. For the first time in my life, evil was no longer a fantasy, like the boogieman, but a terrifying reality.

I Could Have Burned Down My Neighbourhood

Another one of my earliest memories takes me back to a carefree summer spent with a mischievous gang of kids from our neighbourhood. We were a tight-knit group, always seeking adventure and pushing boundaries. Little did we know that our youthful curiosity would lead us to a dangerous encounter that could have had disastrous consequences. I was no more than six years old at this time.

I can't quite recall who first introduced the idea of playing with matches. It might have been me. However, it was Kevin who proudly produced a small box of them from his home, displaying them as if they were a precious treasure. Deep down, we understood that using matches without adult supervision was risky, but that knowledge only added to the allure. We were determined to ignite a fire, oblivious to the potential danger that lay ahead.

We ventured into the wooded area behind my next-door neighbour's house, armed with dried leaves we had collected along the way. Excitement surged through us as we arranged the leaves in a makeshift circle. It felt like we were embarking on an adult endeavour, reminiscent of the scenes from the classic novel *Lord of the Flies*.

I remember trembling as I picked up the matches and tried to strike them against the strip. For a while, either the wooden tip would break off or the match would simply fizzle out on contact with the leaves below. When a match did finally ignite, we watched in awe as the flames danced upon the pile of dry leaves. The speed with which the fire grew startled us; we had given no thought to what would happen next.

Within seconds, the flames roared, reaching a height of two feet. Our exhilaration soon turned to horror as we realized the magnitude of our creation. Panic set in as we recognized we had no means to extinguish the fire, no access to water nearby. Acting on instinct, I grabbed a large slate stone from behind me and dropped it onto the flames, desperately hoping it would be enough to halt the blaze. Fortunately, it did the job.

For a while, we stood there, feeling a collective sense of remorse and guilt as we surveyed the aftermath of our foolish actions—a twisting column of smoke trailing into the sky. Once we were certain that the fire was completely extinguished, we scattered and scurried back to our homes like frightened cockroaches. We barely spoke of the incident for the remainder of that summer, the shock of our near disaster lingering in our minds.

Although catastrophe had been averted, the realization of what might have been weighed heavily on my conscience. As the one who had ignited the match, I carried a deep sense of guilt. It was a defining moment in my young life, an early lesson in the consequences of reckless actions.

From that day forward, whenever a suggestion arose involving danger or forbidden activities, a simple whisper among us was enough to quell the temptation: 'Remember the fire.' Those words served as a powerful reminder, a cautionary tale that prevented us from entertaining other idiotic ideas.

That day, I learned a timeless truth—that wisdom is born from experience, and experience often arises from poor judgment. I was fortunate to have learned this lesson at such an early age; it shielded me from future reckless endeavours.

Afraid of the Dark

One vivid childhood memory I have is of my father playing a game with me and my two brothers when I was just six years old. It involved descending into the dark depths of our basement with the lights out, walking across the vast space, touching the far wall, and returning unscathed. The distance from the stairs to the wall was nearly 60 feet. While the basement itself was a relatively safe and open space, my young imagination was plagued with fears of monsters and unknown terrors lurking in the shadows.

My younger brother, Todd, would go to the bottom of the stairs and return up again. At his age, he was unable to fully comprehend the objective of the game. He was too young to play along.

It was up to my older brother, Mark, and me to face this challenge head-on. Mark, being two years older, more mature, and less fearful, could complete the task effortlessly. I, on the other hand, despite my best efforts could muster the courage only to venture halfway into the pitch-black basement before being overwhelmed by terror and fleeing back to the safety of the stairs. I would claim to have touched the wall, but in truth, I wouldn't have come close.

When my father realized what I was doing, he asked me instead to shout back from where I was standing, and this became how he would measure my progress in the game.

One day, he decided to confront my fear directly. 'Close your eyes, Matt,' he instructed. I complied. 'What do you see?' he asked.

'Nothing,' I replied.

'Is it dark?' he questioned.

'Yes,' I admitted.

'If it's dark, why aren't you afraid now?' he gently probed.

'Because I'm here with you,' I confessed.

'Did you know that being afraid of the dark is nature's way of protecting us from harm?' he said. 'When it's dark, our ancestors used this fear to be extra cautious in the forest or jungle. But down there, you know there is nothing dangerous. I will be with you the entire time, talking to you. I would never ask you to do something that could hurt you. Give it another try, okay?'

Inspired by my father's reassurance, I took a deep breath and descended into the basement once more. Listening to his comforting voice, I pushed forward, step by step. The knowledge that he was by my side, offering unwavering support and ensuring my safety from a distance, helped me overcome my fear. Finally, for the first time, I reached the far wall and joyfully shouted back, 'I'm here! I did it!' I slapped the concrete wall hard with my hand to punctuate this victorious moment.

Instead of immediately returning to the stairs, I stayed in that darkened space. As I relaxed, my anxiety gradually faded away and was replaced by a new-found sense of wonder. It was a pivotal moment in my life that I will forever cherish. It was as if a switch had been flipped, banishing my fear entirely.

This experience taught me a valuable lesson about confronting fear. I began to approach other fears in the same way—pausing to examine what I was truly afraid of and realizing that it was often based on false evidence. I came to understand that FEAR stands for 'False Evidence Appearing Real'. This revelation became my mantra.

I also learned that exposure to fear in controlled doses can gradually reduce anxiety. This process, instilled in me by my father through the basement game, helped me develop the resilience to face, conquer, and harness my fears.

Ultimately, that game in the dark basement became a metaphor for life—a reminder that even in the face of darkness, we can find strength, guidance, and the power to overcome our deepest fears when we have the support of someone we trust.

My Introduction to Dementia

Mrs Connors holds a special place in my heart as my very first customer when I started my first paper route at the age of ten. Because I was so young, my mom accompanied me for the first few months to help collect the subscription fee.

Mrs Connors was a picture of grace, with her gentle demeanour, impeccably styled short grey hair, and elegant attire. Her warm smile and the way she greeted me with a hug each time I arrived to collect payment made me feel truly valued. Sometimes, she would even surprise me with a cookie or a handful of candies, leaving me with a warm glow inside as I left her doorstep.

One day everything changed. As I rang Mrs Connors' doorbell for the usual collection, she opened the door with anger in her eyes. Confusion and hurt welled up within me as she demanded, 'Who are you and what are you doing here?'

Trying to make sense of this unexpected situation, I replied, 'It's me, Matt. I'm your paperboy. You know me. I come here every week.'

Her voice filled with frustration as she shouted, 'You're here to steal from me! I've never seen you before. Get out of here, you thief!'

Bewilderment consumed me as I tried to reason with her, pleading, 'I deliver your paper every day. That's why I'm here on your porch. I would never steal from you.'

Her tone remained harsh as she yelled, 'Leave and never come back, or I'll call the police! Get out of here!'

With tears streaming down my face, I sprinted home to share the painful encounter with my mom. Seeking solace and answers, I said, 'I didn't do anything wrong. Why would she say those awful things to me?' My mom, offering a comforting embrace, paused before gently explaining.

'You did nothing wrong, Matt. Mrs Connors has dementia. It affects her memory and sometimes makes it difficult for her to recognize people. It's something that can happen as people get older. On her good days, she will remember everything, but on her bad days, she may not recognize you, like today. When that happens, try to understand that it's not her true self. Remember her for the person she used to be.'

As mom predicted, there were days when Mrs Connors was herself once more. Those were the days that filled my heart with joy, and I cherished the extra time I spent with her. On her bad days, I would introduce myself repeatedly, hoping for a flicker of recognition. If none came, I would quietly depart, aiming to avoid any further distress.

Encountering such a dramatic change in someone I cared about at such a young age was a jarring and traumatic experience. Gradually, however, I came to accept it as an unfortunate reality of life.

Within a year, Mrs Connors was taken away to a nursing home. Her dementia had reached a point where it was no longer safe for her to live alone. The news of her departure saddened me deeply. I longed to bid her a proper farewell—to express my gratitude for her kindness, warm hugs, and the brightness she brought to my day.

Even after all these years, the memory of Mrs Connors lingers still. She remains a beautiful person in my mind, someone who once held love and compassion for me and countless others.

But the experience also taught me that bad things can happen to good people.

Whatever Happened to Crazy Mrs Heart?

While Mrs Conners had been one of my favourite clients, there was one customer whom I dreaded speaking with during my weekly collections: Mrs Heart. She never had a kind word to say and seemed perpetually angry. Every encounter involved a litany of complaints about the cost of the paper, her neighbours, the weather, and anything else that crossed her mind that day.

Her cantankerous attitude had earned her a reputation among my other customers, who sympathized with my plight. They would often commiserate, saying, 'How is old Mrs Heart? We are so sorry you have to deal with that witch.' Even her closest neighbour, Mrs Templeman, held a deep disdain for her.

Their daily disputes reached epic proportions, often sparked by Mrs Templeman's dog daring to venture into Mrs Heart's lawn to relieve itself. The resulting shouting matches between the two were legendary.

One fateful day, as I approached Mrs Heart's home, I noticed a baby bird on her lawn below the maple tree. It appeared to have fallen from its nest. There was no sign of its mother.

After Mrs Heart opened the door, paid me begrudgingly, and launched into one of her customary tirades, I mustered the courage to inform her about the bird's presence.

'Where is this creature?' she barked.

'It's on the lawn,' I replied, pointing towards it.

Having experienced the full brunt of her fiery temper before, I was apprehensive about what her reaction might be. In fact, I had even prepared myself to swiftly scoop up the bird and retreat if necessary. However, what transpired next took me completely by surprise. Upon laying her eyes on the fragile creature, Mrs Heart's disposition transformed entirely. I could sense a new-found compassion emanating from her.

She asked that I bring the bird inside, and I obliged. Witnessing her tenderness towards the tiny creature was nothing short of awe-inspiring. She gathered a tissue box, gingerly lined it with newspaper, and asked me to fetch some worms from her garden, which I promptly did. Her gentle care for the bird touched my heart deeply.

Later that day, when I visited Mrs Templeman's house, I shared with her the story of the baby bird. As an ardent animal lover, she expressed concern, saying, 'Mrs Heart needs to ensure the food is cut into tiny pieces for the bird's safety. It could harm the little creature. I hope she knows that.' Intrigued by the benevolence her foe had exhibited, Mrs Templeman decided to pay her a visit.

To the astonishment of the entire neighbourhood, Mrs Templeman entered Mrs Heart's house and remained inside for nearly three hours. The sight of these two arch-rivals coming together in such an unprecedented act of camaraderie caused everyone to question if the world order had somehow completely shifted.

The two women worked together to nurse the bird back to health, setting aside their long-standing enmity. But sadly, after three days of their tireless care, the bird died. To console Mrs Heart,

Mrs Templeman sent her a fruit basket, a gesture soon copied by several other neighbours. From that point on, a sense of peace seemed to settle over the neighbourhood. Curious to understand the transformation, one day I asked Mrs Templeman about it.

'Sometimes, people harbour deep losses that manifest as anger and bitterness,' she said. 'We often see only the outward anger without comprehending or understanding the source of the pain within. It was only when I witnessed Mrs Heart's tender care for that bird that I really understood her true nature. After that poor bird died, she cried for hours. It wasn't just for that bird. There was something else there, something much deeper. I could feel that she was suffering from a great loss. I don't know what it was, but I could feel it all around me.'

That day, I learned that a person's pain and sorrow can cause that individual to be angry, anti-social, and withdrawn. I could see that beneath the facade of this crazy old woman, there was a compassionate, caring person who was hurting inside. I often remember this story when I meet others who behave like Mrs Heart used to.

Sadly, the world is filled with many such broken people. Next time you meet one, rather than judging them, try empathy and understanding. You might be surprised to meet the person within.

Understanding Where I Came From

At the age of eleven, a burgeoning curiosity about my heritage ignited a desire within me to learn the German language. After sharing my new passion with my mother, she organized for me to take lessons with one of her friends, an elderly German woman known as Mrs Weber. Excited by the prospect, every Thursday at 4 p.m. I would visit Mrs Weber's grand house atop the hill.

During the first thirty minutes of each session, Mrs Weber would patiently teach me a phrase or two, guiding me through the intricacies of German grammar and pronunciation. Yet, it was the conversations that followed that truly distinguished our encounters. Somehow, she would always find a way to transition into a description of her cherished childhood memories growing up in a small German village.

I would listen with fascination as she regaled me with tales of summers spent frolicking in idyllic landscapes and family excursions to glistening lakes. Even when the stories repeated, I would find myself captivated, envisioning each scene as if it were unfolding before my very eyes. These stories gave me insights into the culture and heritage of my extended family who still lived in Germany.

As our lessons progressed, a transformation took place within Mrs Weber. What began as a serious and reserved ambiance gradually disappeared, giving way to a radiant smile that beamed with enthusiasm. By the end of our sessions, her joy was palpable, leaving an indelible impression upon me.

After a year of these regular encounters, I made the difficult decision to discontinue our lessons. Feeling that my progress in learning the German language was insufficient to justify the time and effort, I informed Mrs Weber and watched the disappointment spread across her face. I couldn't help but feel a pang of regret.

Seven years later, during my senior year in high school, my mother told me the news of Mrs Weber's passing. She asked if I would accompany her to the funeral. I agreed without hesitation. When the day arrived, I saw that only a handful of people had come to pay their respects. Before I could take my seat, a middle-aged woman approached me, her German accent carrying a ring of familiarity.

'Are you Matthew?' she inquired, her gaze meeting mine.

'Yes,' I responded, taken aback.

With a gentle smile, she handed me an aged German book filled with enchanting children's stories. 'This is for you,' she said, presenting the precious tome. 'My great aunt, designated it as part of her will. She often spoke of you throughout the years.'

As her words resonated within me, a wave of confusion surfaced. My own recollections of our shared moments were markedly different.

'I'm amazed that she even remembered me,' I said.

The woman's eyes gleamed with warmth. 'You were a constant presence in her thoughts for many years. She described you as the little German boy searching for his identity and how she played a pivotal role in helping you understand your heritage. During the time you shared with her, your companionship made her very happy.'

In that moment, profound realization coursed through my mind. I came to understand that the act of spending time with an elderly individual could instil in them a deep sense of worth and significance, whether it be through the sharing of wisdom or the mere presence of a companion.

Simultaneously, I came to recognize the personal impact of my time with Mrs Weber. Through her stories and guidance, she illuminated and helped me understand who I truly was.

This experience served as a testament to the power of human connection, the enrichment that arises from intergenerational bonds, and the transformative nature of empathy. Mrs Weber's legacy lives on, not only in the treasured stories she bequeathed to me but also in what she taught me about embracing one's roots and the beauty of shared experiences.

Finn, the Hound from Hell

When I was five years old, an unfortunate incident left a lasting imprint on my young mind: I was bitten in the face by a dog. It was entirely my fault, as I had unknowingly touched its injured tail. In that moment, I came face to face with the raw power of an angry animal and developed a great respect for their potential to harm.

Every week, when I made my way to Mrs Chambers' house to collect payment for the newspaper, I had to confront Finn, the infamous terrorizing dog. Almost without fail, the door would be left ajar, allowing Finn to assert his dominance by jumping up against the screen door, growling and barking ferociously at me. With his deep-set eyes and mixed-breed appearance, I had taken to calling him the 'hound from hell'. The only barrier between his unleashed fury and me was the screen door, against which I would cautiously place my foot to prevent his escape. Each encounter with Finn filled me with terror, yet I had to muster the courage to face this menacing presence.

After ringing the doorbell, I would wait anxiously for Mrs Chambers to shuffle to the door, which would usually take a few minutes. To discipline Finn, she would let out a piercing scream, then slap his snout with a magazine. Finn would yelp in pain and retreat to another room. Only then would Mrs Chambers proceed to pay me for the newspaper. Each time I completed this unsettling ritual, I felt immense relief that I had survived yet another nerve-wracking encounter.

One day, my luck changed as I arrived at Mrs Chambers' door. Finn lunged against it and, to my horror, it swung open wide. Instantly I knew I was in grave danger. Instinctively, I turned and sprinted for my life, with Finn in relentless pursuit, his growls and barks echoing in my ears.

In a desperate bid to escape, I sought refuge in a neighbour's garage. My heart pounded with fear as I scanned the empty space, hoping to find something, anything, with which to defend myself. Alas, it was barren—a hollow sanctuary devoid of any means of protection.

I realized there was no escape from this menacing beast. In that moment of desperation, a memory of my sister's advice echoed in my mind—the best way to tame an angry dog is with kindness. Left with no alternative, I averted my gaze, avoiding direct eye contact with Finn, and cautiously extended my hand before me. Miraculously, the relentless barking ceased. Seizing this glimmer of hope, I inched forward, maintaining my lowered palm.

When I stood a few feet from Finn, I offered my hand for him to sniff. Astonishingly, he responded with curiosity rather than aggression. Encouraged by this breakthrough, I gently reached for the side of his face, tenderly placing my hand on his cheek. In an extraordinary transformation, his demeanour shifted from ferocious to calm. Emboldened by this connection, I rested my other hand on his head and gave a gentle caress. To my astonishment, Finn's tail began to wag—a sign of acceptance and trust. I wondered if his previous aggression stemmed from the repetitive scolding and physical punishment he endured from his owner.

Now, as a friend, I guided Finn back to the waiting arms of his owner, Mrs Chambers, and went on my way. From that moment forward, whenever I approached Mrs Chambers' door, Finn greeted me with a friendly disposition, free from hostility.

Finn 'the horror hound' taught me a timeless truth: kindness has the power to conquer adversity. It transcends barriers, fosters positivity, and defuses negativity, whether in our relationships with animals or humans.

Empathy and understanding can bridge the divides and heal wounds. And even the most ferocious beings can be swayed by compassion.

A Teacher's Compassionate Act

In the fourth grade, our class enjoyed a blissful recess right after lunch—a precious forty minutes of unbridled freedom before our final lessons of the day.

While the playground—encompassing a vast open field and a few basketball courts—was designated as our domain, I seldom abided by the rules. Instead, I would saunter to the edge of the field and, when it looked as if the teachers were not paying attention, I'd venture into the enchanting woods beyond. While I knew this was forbidden, I couldn't help myself. I did it anyway.

For me, nature always held an irresistible allure. I was a great admirer of its magnificent splendour. Within those woods, I would venture to Piper Brook, its tranquil waters teeming with frogs and turtles, or meander to the small swamp, a sanctuary for dragonflies and tadpoles. And there, in the depths of the forest, I would encounter a vibrant tapestry of other life, including snakes, spiders, and an array of other captivating creatures.

To summon us back indoors, two school bells rang—one serving as a gentle reminder, the second a commandment to return to our classrooms.

One day, time seemed to escape my notice as I lost myself in the forest's embrace. I somehow missed hearing both bells. When I finally emerged from my sanctuary, I was greeted by an eerie silence—I was alone on that field.

Hurriedly, I dashed towards the school, only to be intercepted by one of my fourth-grade teachers, her stern gaze signalling trouble. My heart sank, anticipating the dire consequences that would surely await me.

For what felt like an eternity, I sat outside the principal's office, consumed by swirling thoughts—how severe would my punishment be? Would they give me detention? How many days would this be? Would they call my parents?

Finally, the principal emerged, her manner measured yet firm. She motioned me inside with a nod of her head and directed me to a seat beside her desk.

For the next ten minutes, I candidly admitted my transgressions, confessing my clandestine sojourns into the woods and acknowledging the violation of school rules. With a resolute acceptance, I agreed to a week of detention, promising never to repeat my actions. What choice did I have?

As I entered the detention room that first day, a familiar face greeted me—a beloved teacher from the previous year, my favourite companion in third grade. She wore a warm smile as she remarked, 'I heard you got yourself into a bit of trouble again. Oh, Matt, what is it with you? I've been informed about your little escapades in the forest.'

I remained silent, my gaze fixed downward, awaiting my impending fate. I was prepared for the worst.

Unexpectedly, she asked me to follow her. We walked down the main hallway, outside the school, and then crossed the expanse of the field until we reached the edge where the woods awaited. With genuine curiosity, she asked, 'Show me what captivates you in these woods.'

Caught off guard, I hesitated, unsure of how to respond. But then, for the next thirty minutes, I became her guide, leading her to my favourite spots within the forest. I eagerly pointed out the diverse array of animals, the captivating flora, and all the wonders that had captured my young imagination.

Returning to the detention room, she reminded me of the importance of following rules and urged me to explore my passions outside school hours.

But she also thanked me sincerely for the tour and urged me never to cease my search for knowledge.

With those parting words, she presented me with a collection of books celebrating the local flora and fauna, tokens of encouragement and inspiration. She encouraged me to read them to expand my understanding of nature. What had initially appeared as a grave predicament unfolded in an entirely different way.

Years later, this episode became a pivotal moment in my life—one that steered me towards pursuing a degree in biology.

Teachers possess a unique power to shape, guide, and instil self-confidence in their students. This exceptional teacher wielded that power effortlessly, leaving an indelible impact on countless young minds, including my own.

Boe-Man, the Monster

My childhood home was near a small, forested hill called Cedar Mountain. Despite my parents' constant warnings, I continued to venture up the hill all by myself. Their cautionary words only fuelled my curiosity.

Nestled atop the first ridge of the hill was an old sheet metal shack, shrouded in mystery. Nobody knew who—or what—lived within its walls, but the elusive occupant had been given the name 'Boe-Man'.

Now and then, my friends and I would gather the courage to climb the hill, hiding behind a small mound, hoping to catch a glimpse of this hermit-like figure. Although I never met anyone who had truly laid eyes upon Boe-Man, the tales that circulated were enough to send shivers down our spines. Legend had it that he stood a towering eight feet tall, with one arm ominously missing. Rumours spread that he feasted on dogs and survived on tree bark, and his piercing red eyes glowed with an otherworldly intensity. The most haunting story was that he had once abducted a child who was never seen again.

One afternoon, I found myself boasting to my friends about my daring journey up the mountain to seek Boe-Man.

The incredulous looks on their faces made it clear no one believed my audacious claim. One of my friends said no one in their right mind would willingly go up there alone. It was just not done.

But I felt compelled to stand by my story, even though it was a fabrication.

My friend Bobby challenged me, 'If what you say is true, then prove it. Go up there right now and stay at our lookout spot for twenty minutes. I dare you.'

Realizing my reputation was at stake, I reluctantly accepted the dare. I climbed the steep hill, veering past the towering hemlock tree, until I reached the spot from where we used to peer at the enigmatic shack. For twenty agonizing minutes, I lay in wait, observing the metal structure. Having fulfilled my part of the bargain, I turned to leave. But there, standing mere yards behind me, was a middle-aged man. It was Boe-Man in the flesh.

Contrary to the numerous tales I had heard, Boe-Man was not a towering giant, nor did he possess the fiery red eyes of a monster. He appeared to be an ordinary-sized man, with a balding head and a long, silver-streaked beard and hair. Clad in a simple set of blue workman overalls, he exuded an air of humility.

Terrified by the grotesque image my mind had conjured, I panicked, spun around, and dashed away. But my fear led me to trip and fall helplessly to the ground. To my surprise, Boe-Man approached me slowly, his weathered face breaking into a warm smile, as he extended his hand to lend me aid.

My mind raced with conflicting emotions. I feared that this stranger might intend to abduct me, so I sprung to my feet once more, darting down the path to safety.

When I reached the bottom of the hill, my friends awaited me. Despite my earnest retelling of the encounter, they dismissed my words as fiction. They couldn't fathom that I truly had ventured to our lookout spot alone, even less that I had met the monster face to face. The idea was beyond belief.

In many ways, that encounter with Boe-Man became a pivotal moment in my life. It was the first time I realized that we are often fed stories that bear no resemblance to the truth. Boe-Man, the fearsome monster of Cedar Mountain, was nothing more than an elderly, homeless man residing in a humble shack. He shattered the illusions that had held me captive, much like Santa Claus and the Easter Bunny would in the years to come.

Mr Barnes, My Dear Friend

I had the great privilege of meeting Mr Barnes when he was in his late seventies, living alone in a charming house nestled at the corner where three roads converged. As his paperboy for several years, I developed a unique bond with this solitary man.

Every Thursday, during my visit to collect the subscription fee, Mr Barnes would graciously invite me into his home. After retrieving the money, he would kindly inquire if I had a moment to spare. Without hesitation, I always accepted. We would settle down, and that's when the magic began.

Mr Barnes would approach his desk, selecting an item of seemingly ordinary nature but with immense sentimental value. It could be a key chain from his early days as a used car salesman, an old fountain pen that once signed his very first personal cheque, or a tattered business card bearing his name. Though these mundane artifacts seemed unremarkable at first glance, he possessed an extraordinary ability to weave enchanting tales around them. With a mixture of drama, humour, and sometimes even a touch of mystery, he captivated my eleven-year-old imagination. Through his storytelling prowess, he turned the ordinary into something truly extraordinary.

Mr Barnes never spoke of having a family, and it was evident that he led a solitary existence, with few friends to keep him company. Yet, our friendship was unwavering and strong.

Among his treasured possessions, one item stood out above the rest—a military medal he had received during World War II. He would never divulge the details of his heroic actions that garnered him this honour, but whenever he spoke of it, his gaze would drift away, as if he could physically hold the medal between his fingers and be transported back in time.

One day, he surprised me by placing his medal in my hands. He then said it was now mine. It represented a gesture of utmost generosity and trust, a testament to the friendship we had forged over the years. I was taken aback, overwhelmed by this act of kindness. Along with the medal, he gave me a $2 tip, a sum far beyond anything he had gifted me before. For a young paperboy, it felt like a small fortune.

Three days later, I made a startling discovery. The newspaper I had delivered the previous day still lay untouched on Mr Barnes' porch. Concern gnawed at my heart as I pondered the reason for his absence. On the fourth day, a woman arrived at his doorstep, delivering the tragic news. Mr Barnes had succumbed to heart disease, choosing to spend his final moments in the comfort of his own home.

That day, I was left grappling with a mixture of grief and confusion. Why hadn't he confided in me about his illness? Why hadn't he given me the chance to bid him farewell? Anger and frustration swelled within me, as I yearned for the opportunity to express my gratitude for his vivid stories, to convey how much I had learned from him, and to demonstrate my care and concern as a true friend.

It was my first encounter with death and it left me speechless for a while. But as time passed, I began to understand Mr Barnes' actions. Two years later, another customer invited me into her home, explaining that she had something to offer me. Alarm bells rang in my mind, and I immediately voiced my concern for her well-being.

At first, she denied that anything was wrong. Then, after some coaxing, she finally confided that she had been diagnosed with pancreatic cancer.

In that moment, a thought crystallized within me. I realized that as people approach the end of their lives, the act of leaving special gifts for those they care about holds immense significance. It is a sign we can all watch out for among the people we hold dear. I couldn't help but imagine myself doing the same when my own time drew near.

Mr Barnes, in his quiet wisdom, had bestowed upon me more than just his beloved military medal. He had imparted an invaluable life lesson—a reminder of the importance of genuine connections, of sharing stories, and of leaving behind tokens of love and appreciation. Though I wished for a different ending to our story, his death left an indelible mark on my soul.

Now, as I reflect upon those bittersweet memories, I carry forward the legacy of Mr Barnes, determined to make a difference in the lives of those around me.

And when my time comes to bid farewell to this world, I can be sure that the moments we shared will be forever remembered and cherished, for I too shall leave behind heartfelt gifts.

It Always Seems Impossible Until It Happens

One summer, when I was eleven years old, I yearned for a brand new bicycle. The one I had was worn out, with a flat tyre and a chain that stubbornly refused to stay on the gears. Excitedly, I approached my parents and asked if I could get a new bike. To my dismay, they said I would have to wait until Christmas, many months away.

Without a functioning bike, I decided to walk to the centre of my town. Halfway to my destination, something miraculous happened—I spotted a crumpled $5 bill lying on the ground. It was the first time I had ever stumbled upon paper money, and at that time, it felt like discovering a small fortune. Buoyed by this stroke of luck, I continued my journey and soon came across a garage sale taking place in someone's front yard.

Clutching the $5 bill in my hand, I ventured eagerly into the array of second-hand goods. To my amazement, my eyes landed on a vibrant red Schwinn bike. Though it appeared too big for me, I couldn't resist the urge to try it out. Much to my delight, as I hopped onto the bike, I realized it was a perfect fit. Excitement surged through me; I couldn't believe my luck. The owner told me that the price was $40 but could possibly be negotiated down to $30 if I was genuinely interested.

Alas, that was still far beyond my means, so I reluctantly placed the bike back among the other items. However, as I continued browsing, something else caught my attention—an intriguing high school chemistry set. Although the details on the box and the instructions inside seemed way beyond my comprehension, I felt drawn towards it.

The price tag read $10—within my limited budget—so I gathered the courage to make an offer. Holding up my five-dollar bill, I asked the owner if he would consider accepting it. His gaze met mine, and after a moment of contemplation, he spoke, 'Alright, but promise me you won't experiment with any of these chemicals without proper adult supervision. It could be dangerous. Will you promise me you will first show this to your mom and dad?'

Eager to seize the opportunity, I gladly made the promise. I handed over my $5, exchanged a grateful smile with the owner, and continued my journey towards the town centre, chemistry set in hand.

As I stepped into the familiar Thrifty Drug Store to get a bag of M&M candies, the original destination of my trip into town, Mr Martin, the pharmacist, approached me with curiosity, intrigued by my new-found possession.

Taking a closer look at the test tubes and various chemicals, Mr Martin's face lit up with nostalgic recognition. He exclaimed, 'I had the exact same chemistry set twenty years ago. This brings back so many fond memories.' His enthusiasm was contagious. I couldn't help but feel a glimmer of excitement myself.

Curiously, he pointed to a large brown bottle filled with powder and asked, 'Do you know what this is?' I shook my head. With a twinkle in his eye, he revealed, 'It's silver nitrate. If you dissolve it in water and add a copper penny, the silver nitrate will react with the copper, producing silver crystals. Given the current price of silver, this could be worth quite a sum.'

Suddenly, a thrilling possibility surfaced before me. Emboldened by Mr Martin's evident interest, I asked sheepishly, 'Would you be interested in buying this from me?' His eyes widened, and after a moment of consideration, he asked, 'How much?' Without hesitation, I confidently responded, 'Thirty dollars.' To my delight, Mr Martin readily agreed, and we sealed the deal with a handshake.

I returned to the yard sale and there it was—that beautiful red bike. Within minutes it was mine.

Life sometimes has a peculiar way of surprising us. I had begun the day with nothing but ended up seizing an opportunity and riding home on a new bike.

Time and chance happen to all of us. I believe that if we remain open to the potential for good things to occur, then they often do.

On that memorable summer day, as an eleven-year-old with a five-dollar bill and an unyielding spirit, I experienced first-hand the power of embracing the unexpected and making the most of the opportunities that followed.

I Was Alone in the Forest with an Injured Foot

It was a cold winter day when I made the decision to hike up Cedar Mountain. Despite the murmurs of an impending snow blizzard, there were no visible signs of it yet. That year in winter, I had been cautioned repeatedly against venturing up the mountain alone, especially during the winter months. But since I was overcome by boredom and the absence of my friends, I decided to go anyway.

With a clear objective in mind, I climbed the steep hill along the main pathway until I reached the open clearing. From there, I left the beaten track, opting to go through the woods to save time. My destination lay on the western side of the mountain—an old farmer's field, patiently awaiting my exploration. While it was bitter cold that day, as long as I kept moving, I felt warm enough.

As I trekked through the serene forest, halfway to my destination, delicate snowflakes began their graceful descent. I paused, mesmerized by their glistening, ethereal beauty. Moments later, the pace of snowfall and an uncomfortable realization hit me. Being in the woods during a severe snowstorm, off the main path, could be dangerous. Hastening my pace, I trudged forward with a keen sense of urgency.

Regrettably, fate had a cruel twist in store. While navigating the treacherous terrain, I miscalculated my step and twisted my ankle. Pain coursed through me, and I collapsed onto the ground. Panic seized me as I attempted to stand, only to fall repeatedly in agony.

Suddenly I realized the danger I was in. I was stranded deep within the woods, unable to walk, and not a single person was even aware of my impromptu adventure. For a time, fear and despair gripped me as tears welled up and fell down my cheeks. Desperation mingled with the biting cold, intensifying my feeling of dread. I closed my eyes and prayed for a miracle.

When I opened them, I noticed a fallen branch lying beside me, several feet away. This gave me a flicker of hope. If the wood proved sturdy, I could fashion it into a makeshift crutch. Encouraged by this strategy, I painstakingly manoeuvred towards the branch, breaking off a few side branches to create a functional support.

Leaning on my improvised crutch, I began a laborious journey towards the field. Each step was a test of resilience, where maintaining my balance ensured relief from the searing pain. The progress was painstakingly slow, but I was determined to reach my destination.

After I had covered a considerable distance, nearly 500 feet from the main path, I noticed some people up ahead. Hope flickered once more. It was a young couple walking their dog.

But to my dismay, despite my repeated calls for help, they only glanced in my direction before turning back and continuing their walk.

Bewildered, I pressed on, and after what seemed like an eternity, I finally reached the animal shelter near the field. Trembling and exhausted, I used their phone to dial my mother's number. After she arrived, she inspected my injured foot and reprimanded me for my reckless solo expedition. I listened attentively to her admonishment, fully aware of the truth in her words. I had to admit my actions had been foolish and irresponsible, potentially endangering my own life.

Yet, in that moment, the scolding was overshadowed by a feeling of relief. I couldn't help but recall the terror and the fear that I might never make it home again. At that instant, the overriding emotion was immense gratitude for being safe and alive.

Sometimes, it takes a harrowing experience like this to remind us of how precious life really is. In hindsight, that wintry day taught me about the importance of responsible decision-making and to avoid choices that jeopardize my well-being. It was an important lesson we all must learn, not only for the sake of ourselves, but for all those who care about us.

I Stood There and Just Watched

Brian was always a little different from most kids. With a perpetual smile on his face, he exuded an endearing goofiness that set him apart from his peers. It was his unique brand of happiness that drew me to him when we first met in Cub Scouts. While others found his fascination with space, NASA, Star Trek, and all things nerdy peculiar, I found them intriguing. Soon enough, we became friends.

Amidst a pack of rowdy and loud scouts, Brian stood out as soft-spoken and considerate. He never had a negative word to say about anyone and possessed an innate goodness that radiated from within. It was clear to me that he was a genuinely good person.

When I transitioned from Cub Scouts to Boy Scouts, I urged Brian to join me. However, he felt that he wouldn't excel in the Boy Scouts, partly because of the physical demands. So reluctantly, we went our separate ways and lost touch over time—I pursued my passion for music in the band, while Brian explored his love for drama.

One afternoon, just before the start of summer break, an unusual commotion in the playground caught my attention. What I witnessed shook me to the core. There, in the midst of a baying crowd, Brian stood, bearing the brunt of taunts and teasing from two of the notorious bullies that plagued our school. The scene was heartbreaking, but what was even more disheartening was the fact that no one, including myself, came forward to help him.

I couldn't escape the irony of the situation. Having experienced bullying myself, I intimately understood the agony of isolation and the humiliation of being a spectacle for others. Yet, despite our previous friendship, I found myself frozen, just another bystander amidst the sea of onlookers.

At one pivotal moment, our eyes met, and I glimpsed a plea for help in Brian's gaze. He yearned for me to intervene, to lend him the support he desperately needed.

Regrettably, I turned away, consumed by a paralyzing sense of shame. Though I longed to do the right thing, my fear and desire to fit in eclipsed my courage. I was too weak to defy the prevailing current and stand up against the bullies.

By this point in my life, I already understood the complex dynamics surrounding the confrontation of bullies. I knew that speaking out against them often came at a personal cost, as it often redirected their negative energy towards the intervenor. I also understood that the bully was unlikely to be dissuaded by a simple admonishment; instead, their rage would turn towards the one who dared to challenge them. This awareness, however, did little to assuage the guilt I felt when reflecting upon that fateful incident. Looking back, I wish I had found the personal strength within myself to act, to be the friend Brian needed.

But life moved forward, and I never saw Brian again. When we entered junior high school, he was conspicuously absent. Did he transfer to another school? Did he relocate? The answers remained forever elusive.

Today, as an advocate for justice and the rights of others, I strive to stand up for what is right and just. I have learned from my past, and I refuse to let fear dictate my actions. Yet, the remorse I carry for letting down my friend remains a regret that lingers deep within me. It serves as a constant reminder of the person I once was—one who lacked the fortitude to act when it mattered most. Though I cannot change the past, I can only hope that my present and future actions help to compensate for my past shortcomings.

I Won? Me? Really?

From my earliest memories, there was always an undeniable urge within me to move swiftly from place to place. I loved to run. Even in my primary school days, the moment the final bell rang, I would set off on a race home, covering approximately 2.4 kilometres. I was driven by a relentless desire to complete my tasks ahead of schedule.

As a primary school kid, I took on the responsibility of two paper routes. Each day, six days a week, I would embark on a mission to deliver a staggering seventy papers throughout my neighbourhood. Laden with bags filled to the brim, I darted from one house to another, a reflection of the fictional character Forrest Gump, who ceaselessly ran through life.

My main motivation for my frenetic pace was my devotion to catch my favourite show, the original Star Trek series, airing precisely at 4 p.m. every weekday. Despite having watched every episode countless times, the thought of missing even a single instalment was unthinkable to me. It became one of the few rituals that I faithfully observed.

As the end of fifth grade loomed near, our primary school unveiled a grand exercise campaign, aimed at inspiring young individuals to embrace physical fitness. To further incentivize our participation, the school devised a contest to determine who could accumulate the greatest running mileage each month. In my typical fashion, I paid little attention to this initiative, casually filling out the form indicating my daily running distance and submitting it without a second thought.

One day during the final week of school, an assembly was held, encompassing the entire student body. It was not only a gathering for collective end-of-year announcements but also an occasion to give out awards. Absorbed in my daydreams, I was abruptly jolted from my trance when the girl sitting beside me frantically shook my arm and whispered, 'They just called your name! Hurry up, you need to go up on stage!'

Confusion clouded my mind as I glanced up to find all eyes fixed upon me. What had I done? Why was I being summoned? Initially, a sense of apprehension gripped me, fearing that I might be in some sort of trouble. Nevertheless, I navigated through the sea of students and walked up on the stage to meet the principal, uncertain of what awaited me.

Without delay, the principal extended her hand, a smile of genuine pride illuminating her face as she presented me with a trophy, lauding my achievement. 'Congratulations, Matthew!' she exclaimed. 'You have secured the top prize for running the most miles among all students in the school. While most of your peers recorded around 16 kilometres per month, you astonishingly ran over 214 kilometres. Outstanding!'

I was awestruck, standing there in disbelief as I stepped off the stage. Never once had it occurred to me that my penchant for running set me apart from others. I had simply assumed that everyone shared my fervour for swift movement.

For the first time in my young life, I was being recognized for something I had achieved. The feeling was an unexpected delight, a surge of validation coursing through my veins. So great was that feeling that I felt inspired to strive for even greater achievements. I was hooked on success.

I learned then that even the smallest token of acknowledgment can be a catalyst in propelling us to greater heights and boosting our self-worth.

I also learned the importance of acknowledging and celebrating the accomplishments of others. Awards and accolades, no matter how modest, can uplift and motivate us. They are like beacons of encouragement, guiding us towards our future triumphs.

Why Didn't He Blow the Horn?

During the summer before entering the sixth grade, my friends and I had a weekly ritual of venturing over to the train tracks near the Cashway Lumber Yard. We would eagerly await the rumbling trains, armed with a handful of pennies to place on the tracks. The thrill of retrieving those flattened coins after a train had passed over them became one of our favourite pastimes during the languid days of summer. On fortunate occasions, we would see up to five trains whisking by.

However, there came a day when the tracks fell quiet. Sitting there with my friends, Scott and Neil, I couldn't help but think of the adage that a watched pot never boils. Determined to tempt fate, I proposed we should sit on the tracks but avert our gaze in both directions. I confidently reassured them, 'If we avoid looking, the train will surely come.'

'But what if a train actually does come?' Neil said, his uncertainty and concern palpable.

'They always blow their horn when they spot people on the tracks,' I countered, brimming with conviction.

Scott and Neil remained sceptical, but reluctantly agreed. And so, for forty-five minutes, we engaged in lively conversation, facing one another as if trying to deceive the universe into believing our disinterest.

'It's been quite a while. I don't think I want to continue,' Neil admitted, a hint of fear in his voice.

'No, we must stick to the plan. We'll hear the train approaching from miles away,' I urged, determined to maintain our pact.

Then, in a sudden burst of alarm, Neil finally turned to the right and exclaimed, 'There's a train coming!'

Reacting swiftly, Scott also swivelled his head and cried out, 'Train!' He instinctively leaped away from the tracks.

I felt their synchronized revelation was attempting to lure me into caving in, but I stood resolute. *I won't fall for your ploy*, I thought defiantly.

Seeing my scepticism, Scott seized my head firmly, and forcibly directed my gaze towards the track. There, a mere 500 feet away, a colossal red freight train was hurtling towards us.

The shock coursed through my veins, causing my legs to buckle and nearly surrender beneath me. With a hair's breadth of time remaining, I propelled myself off the tracks. The train roared past us, thunderously, a menacing reminder of the peril that had loomed just moments before.

'Why didn't the train blow its horn?' I said, trembling and bewildered. Despite its great size and speed, I still didn't hear it coming.

Looking back, I pondered the possibilities. Perhaps the train conductor was momentarily distracted, or maybe they simply believed that we would get out of the way.

Alas, we may never know the truth. But to this day, I have nightmares of trains relentlessly pursuing me.

It is one of the many narrow escapes and reckless exploits that peppered my childhood. From car crashes to a daring confrontation with a knife-wielding teenager during my time as a camp counsellor, I embraced a life brimming with risks. In those days, I wore the moniker 'Savage' with a sense of pride, blissfully unaware of the shudders that such recollections would evoke in me now.

But as we grow older, such harrowing experiences tend to imprint on one's consciousness the importance of safety.

Fast-forward to my tenure as a parent and I have undergone a profound transformation.

Consumed by an almost obsessive desire to protect my children from harm, I shun any hint of perilous activities. Perhaps deep within, I fear that my kids might inherit my inclination for recklessness.

Looking back, I realize now that balance was the key. While my past escapades remain cautionary tales, I recognize the value of fostering resilience and calculated risk-taking in my children's lives.

Ultimately, through a delicate balancing act of safety and exploration, I have tried to teach them the wisdom I gleaned from my own hair-raising journeys.

Let It Die

As a child, one of the greatest joys of visiting the beach was strolling along the jetty to observe the fishermen and their bountiful catches. I possessed a fascination with sharks. I devoured books about them, sketched intricate drawings of their majestic forms, and yearned for any opportunity to catch a glimpse of these captivating creatures.

On one visit, about thirty minutes after my arrival at the beach, an experienced angler began to reel in his catch. Intrigued, I stood transfixed, anticipation coursing through my veins. As the object of his efforts emerged from the water, a series of expletives tumbled from the fisherman's lips. 'Another damn shark,' he muttered, his frustration palpable.

Yet, despite his irritation, I couldn't contain my excitement at the sight of this eighteen-inch marvel being drawn closer to the shore. While seeing any fish being caught held its own allure, witnessing a shark surfacing before my eyes was an unexpected thrill, a rare spectacle.

Once the fisherman had removed the hook from this creature, an unthinkable act unfolded before me. Instead of releasing it back into the water, he callously tossed the shark between the unforgiving rocks of the jetty. Recognizing the impending demise of this helpless creature, an urge to rescue it surged within me. However, before I could act, he sternly barked, 'Leave that thing alone. Those are trash fish; they devour my bait. Let it die.'

Refusing to accept such a fate for this defenceless fish, I initially disregarded his words and prepared to reach down and retrieve the creature. Angered by my defiance, the man growled, 'I told you to leave that shark where it is. I caught it, so it is mine to do with as I please. Now get out of here.'

Paralyzed by the weight of his authority, I felt powerless and conflicted. He was an adult, while I was merely a child. I reluctantly acquiesced, my gaze fixated upon the dying creature, its struggles gradually diminishing. Five agonizing minutes later, the fisherman, dissatisfied with his unfruitful spot, rose, and ventured further along the jetty in search of better prospects.

Seizing the moment when his back was turned, I gingerly manoeuvred myself down amidst the jagged rocks, desperately striving to secure a hold on the shark's tail. No longer thrashing about, it lay still, its life hanging by a thread. Despite my best efforts to squeeze down past the rocks, the task proved arduous, almost insurmountable.

Realizing time was of the essence, I expelled all the air from my lungs and summoned every ounce of strength within me to push my body forward. Finally, against all odds, my fingers clutched the shark's tail. With an acute sense of urgency, I climbed out from the treacherous space until I reached the top. And then, with a mixture of hope and anguish, I cast the shark back into the ocean. My heart shattered as I watched it overturn and float helplessly, its belly exposed to the world. I was too late.

That day, anger welled up within me. Why did that innocent creature have to meet such a senseless demise? It had no say in being a shark—it simply existed, following the instincts engrained within its very being.

I share this story not to dwell on a solitary fish, but to underscore the impact it had on my young self. In that moment, I vowed to never again allow anyone or anything to hinder me from doing what I believed was right. To me, it was a matter of life or death for an innocent being. And in retrospect, I realized that I should have seized the fish and defiantly cast it into the ocean, regardless of the man's protests. What would he have done to me? Perhaps nothing.

Sometimes, unexpected encounters in life possess the power to illuminate our true character and reinforce our values. This was undeniably one of those transformative instances. If I could relive that day, I would ensure the survival of that fragile fish. It was a lesson learned—a reminder of the importance of standing up for what we believe in, even in the face of opposition.

I Stood There Feeling like a Fraud

During my days as a young Cub Scout, one eagerly anticipated event stood out among the rest—the exhilarating Pinewood Derby race. For those unacquainted with this spirited competition, imagine Cub Scouts racing small, gravity-powered wooden cars down a sloped track. It was an opportunity for scouts not only to forge stronger bonds with their parents but to experience the thrill of competition and savour the sweet taste of accomplishment.

However, I must confess that, contrary to popular belief, the Pinewood Derby was not a source of enjoyment for me. While my father was rarely present during my scouting adventures, he seemed to make up for it when it came to this event. Taking full control of the process, he would seize the block of wood and single-handedly design the car.

Each year, I would timidly express my desire to take part in the building process, but his smile would dismiss my plea as he would pose the question, 'Don't you want to win the race or create the most original looking car design?' To my honest reply of 'No,' he would shrug his shoulders and simply forge ahead, undeterred.

As a scientist, he would utilize every scientific principle and design strategy to make the car sleek, aerodynamic, and visually striking. Although victory in the race usually eluded us, we often won trophies for the car's aesthetics.

Standing on that stage, accepting my award, I couldn't shake the feeling of being a fraud—knowing deep down that it wasn't my craftsmanship that had won it. I sensed similar sentiments among my fellow scouts.

Years later, when my own children joined the Cub Scouts, my son, Brandon, arrived home with his Pinewood Derby car kit. Excitement raced through me as I seized the opportunity I had long yearned for. Without hesitation, I unpacked the kit, brimming with plans to create a remarkable car. I scoured the internet for optimal designs, seeking the ideal combination of speed and aesthetic appeal. Finally, the moment arrived—I was about to construct my very first Pinewood Derby car!

That first year, I meticulously crafted the car, and our efforts yielded fourth place in the speed category, accompanied by an award for the best-looking car. I had triumphed.

The following year, when Brandon approached me once again, I was brimming with confidence. Equipped with fresh design ideas and new-found knowledge about speed-boosting techniques, I was primed for success. Yet, just as I began preparing my tools, Brandon approached me with a heartfelt plea. 'Dad, I'm supposed to build this car myself. It's my project. Can I please have the car kit? Please?'

In that moment, a flashback to my own negative experiences washed over me; I was a boy once again, standing idly by while my father carried out my work. Realizing that history was repeating itself, I relinquished my grandiose plans of constructing a supercar and passed the baton to Brandon.

Though his creation appeared modest compared to the intricate designs of some of the other boys, it possessed an inexplicable swiftness. Brandon secured second place for overall speed—a triumph entirely of his own making. Witnessing his pride in his accomplishment, I, too, swelled with joy.

That day, an invaluable lesson reverberated within me—allowing children to undertake their own projects is paramount. It is through this that they develop the skills and discernment they need to navigate the complexities of life.

In the end, I had discovered the true essence of the Pinewood Derby. It was a shared journey of growth and self-discovery between a parent and child. And as I watched Brandon bask in the glory of his achievement, I realized that fostering a child's independence is the only way to prepare them for their life to come.

Facing a Childhood Bully

Since the day I first encountered Jeff at Boy Scouts, he singled me out for torment. He was the first bully I had ever met, a senior scout perched atop the social hierarchy who seemed fixated on making my life unbearable. His presence loomed large at our weekly meetings, where he delighted in taunting and physically intimidating me, while my pacifist nature prevented me from retaliating. Throughout the first eight months of my Boy Scouts journey, his unwavering hostility cast a dark shadow over my experiences.

However, amidst the tumult, there existed a single arena where my assertive spirit found an unexpected outlet—dodgeball. This high-energy game, often played after our meetings, unlocked a dormant ferocity within me. As soon as I grasped the ball, an internal switch flipped, propelling me into a frenzy. Spinning aggressively, I would fire projectiles upon my opponents without mercy, relishing the competitive fervour that permeated the air. It was a whirlwind of balls, dodges, and victorious eliminations.

One evening, Jeff and I found ourselves on opposing dodgeball teams. Within moments, the battlefield narrowed, reducing us to the sole contenders. An opportunity for retribution materialized—a chance to settle the score for the myriad wrongs he had inflicted upon me. Poised for redemption, I bided my time, awaiting Jeff's move.

He feigned shots repeatedly, adding an impish dance to his repertoire, aimed at distracting me. Just as he finally released the ball, he collapsed dramatically to the ground. His aim missed me by a hair's breadth; I remained in the game. Seizing the moment, I clenched the ball tightly, drew back my arm, and launched it towards him with unbridled force, my heart pulsating with anticipation of victory.

Unexpectedly, Jeff swiftly pivoted, snatched the ball from mid-air, and retaliated with a lightning-quick throw. Caught off guard, the ball struck the side of my head, causing me to lose my balance and crumple to the ground, clutching my ear in agony. In that moment, disappointment washed over me as my grand opportunity for revenge evaporated into thin air. Once again, Jeff had emerged triumphant. The story of my life.

But then, something extraordinary happened. Jeff sprinted towards me; a look of genuine concern etched across his face. 'Are you okay?' he asked, visibly shaken. 'I'm so sorry. I didn't mean to throw it so hard. I truly am sorry.'

Puzzled, I marvelled at this unexpected display of empathy. What had happened to the aggressive, obnoxious, and antagonistic senior scout I knew? It appeared as though he had suddenly become aware of the boundaries he had crossed. In that instant, I caught a glimpse of another facet of his character.

Remarkably, following this pivotal 'dodgeball incident,' our relationship underwent a transformation. Jeff's attitude changed from hostility to protectiveness and even support. There were even instances when I felt confident enough to tell him to stop his brutish behaviour towards younger scouts; even more astonishingly, he heeded my plea.

I learned an important lesson that day. That sometimes, we fail to witness the entirety of a person until circumstances reveal their hidden depths. Both goodness and darkness reside in each of us, awaiting a catalyst to be set free.

What Goes Around, Comes Around

My best friend Mark and I were pedalling our bikes up a steep hill in our tranquil neighbourhood when our attention was abruptly drawn to an unusual sight. Standing in the middle of the road, clad in pyjamas, was an elderly man. He appeared confused and disoriented.

We halted our bikes and approached him cautiously. 'Are you okay?' I asked with genuine concern.

He looked bewildered. 'I can't seem to find the newspaper. I went searching for it, but now I'm lost.'

'Where do you live?' Mark asked, hoping to unravel the mystery of his predicament.

Surveying his surroundings, the elderly man's eyes filled with uncertainty, and he confessed, 'I don't know. I can't seem to find my way back home.'

Instantly, we decided on a plan of action. Mark would pedal back to his house, informing his mother of the situation, and asking her to contact the police. Drawing from my previous encounter with

Mrs Conners, who had dementia, the signs pointed to a similar condition afflicting this man.

As Mark rode off to seek help, the disoriented man reached out, clutching my hand with a trembling grip. Anxiousness coursed through me, but I instinctively began to share information about myself—I told him my name, age (a mere twelve years), and residence on Knollwood Road. Not knowing what else to do, I continued speaking about various aspects of my life, recounting tales of my paper route, Boy Scouts adventures, and friendships at school.

He gazed at me, riveted, and remained silent throughout my soliloquy.

Within minutes, a police car pulled up, and to my relief, it was Officer Morgan, a familiar face from my neighbourhood. He approached the man with great compassion, inquiring about his name, only to be met with silence. Undeterred, Officer Morgan probed further, asking if he lived nearby, to which the man shook his head.

Having explained the situation, Officer Morgan decided to knock on the nearest house for assistance. A woman answered the door, pointing him in the direction of the hill. He then returned to me and asked, 'Can you stay with him a little longer?' Naturally, I agreed.

After a brief interval, Officer Morgan returned, accompanied by a middle-aged woman. She tenderly clasped her father's hand and enveloped him in a warm embrace. Unsure of my role at that moment, I discreetly made my exit, retracing my steps back home to join my friend so we could continue on our way.

Two years passed, and I found myself embarking on my maiden entrepreneurial endeavour—selling seeds door-to-door. Intrigued by an advertisement in *Boys' Life* magazine, I eagerly signed up, yearning to achieve the coveted top prize of a face mask, snorkel, and fins by selling forty seed packets priced at a humble 50 cents each. Acquiring these items was a dream I had nurtured for years.

Knocking on doors, I mustered the courage to present my sales pitch, only to face rejection at every turn. However, when I arrived at the eleventh house, I was greeted with a radiant smile.

The middle-aged woman who answered the door seemed pleased to see me, a stark difference from my other attempts. Intrigued, I commenced my spiel, and to my astonishment, she made an unexpected proposition. 'How much would it cost to purchase all the seeds?' she inquired.

'Twenty dollars,' I replied, momentarily taken aback by her potential interest.

Without hesitation, she handed me a crisp $20 bill and confided, 'Do you remember me?'

Confusion clouded my mind as I responded truthfully, 'No.'

A gentle smile graced her lips as she shared her heartfelt recollection, 'A couple of years ago, you and your friend came to the aid of my father. He had wandered off, and you called the police.'

I nodded earnestly. 'I remember. How is he?'

Her expression softened, and she replied with a touch of sorrow, 'He passed away last November. However, I clearly remember your kindness on that day. So, with these seeds, I plan to honour his memory by planting flowers and vegetables in his name.'

In that moment, I couldn't help but think of the age-old adage, 'What goes around, comes around.'

I Never Would've Survived Fifth Grade without him

From the very first day I encountered Mr Ryan, my fifth-grade teacher, his character spread kindness, patience, and unwavering encouragement. Unfortunately, such positive experiences were rare for me when it came to my previous primary school teachers.

I must confess, during my early years, I was an exuberant and hyperactive child—a bundle of uncontainable energy. At that time, there wasn't a specific label for a child like me who struggled to concentrate for extended periods. Now, with the recognition of ADHD, I can confidently say that was me.

The initial periods of each school day were relatively uneventful, but as time wore on, my mind would inevitably begin to wander. I yearned for moments of excitement, preferring lively conversations, aimless walks, and jovial antics over the monotonous routine of a structured classroom. My previous teachers responded to my behaviour with frequent punishments and swift trips to the principal's office for daring to speak out of turn. Back then, I was a frequent visitor to the detention room after school.

I distinctly recall one of my fourth-grade teachers sternly cautioning me on the very first day of class, 'Matthew, I hope you plan on behaving in my class. I've heard about your reputation. Don't cause any trouble.' From that moment on, I became the designated 'troublemaker' within the class.

But Mr Ryan, he was different. From the very beginning, he seemed to possess an innate understanding of me. Whenever my attention wandered, he would call upon me, inviting me to share my thoughts on the subject at hand. Instead of challenging me, his warm smile communicated unwavering support and genuine interest.

Initially, I felt apprehensive and uncertain when he sought my input during class discussions. Yet, as time passed, I realized that he encouraged my participation not only to maintain my focus but also to honour my unique perspective. It became a source of enjoyment rather than a cause for anxiety.

On occasion, Mr Ryan would request my assistance in organizing the classroom. For fifteen precious minutes after class, I would diligently tidy up papers, arrange chairs, and engage in heartfelt conversations with him. He would inquire about my day, genuinely interested in how I was faring. It was the first time a teacher had treated me with respect instead of constantly reprimanding me.

When a position opened in the audio-visual club, Mr Ryan personally approached me, asking if I would be interested. Without hesitation, I accepted the opportunity. This role allowed me to step out of the confines of the classroom and take charge of setting up projectors when films were to be shown. It bestowed upon me a sense of purpose, responsibility, and belonging.

Curiosity eventually got the better of me, and I mustered the courage to ask Mr Ryan why he showed me such kindness. In response, a warm smile played upon his lips as he uttered words that would resonate with me for years to come. 'Because you possess a spirited heart, Matthew. It is a unique trait, and I want to help nurture it.'

At the time, I struggled to fully comprehend his message. But as the years passed, I began to realize that perhaps Mr Ryan had experienced a similar journey during his own childhood. I couldn't help but wonder.

As I turned thirty, a desire to express my gratitude to Mr Ryan ignited within me. I longed to find him to convey just how significant his presence had been in my life. Alas, this was an era before the advent of the internet. My search for his contact details was unsuccessful.

If only I had been able to find him, I would have told him the immense importance he held in my life. His unwavering belief in me had fostered my self-confidence. His kindness had touched my heart and bestowed upon me a sense of optimism for the future.

The qualities of a remarkable teacher include exceptional communication skills, attentive listening, a collaborative spirit, adaptability, empathy, and boundless patience. When these attributes are used to help a student yearning for guidance, remarkable things can occur. Mr Ryan was the guiding force that steered my life onto the right path. For me, it was nothing less than a metamorphosis.

Mrs Newton

When I was twelve years old, I had a newspaper route on Augusta Drive, the street adjacent to mine. My daily routine involved delivering papers in the afternoons to around twenty-five homes. During the weekends, I would collect the subscription fees.

Among these houses, there was one that always made me hesitate—Mrs Newton's. Each time I approached her home, I knew what to expect. She would invariably ask for a favour, whether it was moving a stack of newspapers or reaching for something high on a shelf. Following that, she'd engage me in conversation for what seemed like an eternity, discussing trivial matters that I couldn't care less about. I couldn't help but see it as a chore, as all I wanted was to complete my job and return home.

One afternoon, I confided in my mother about my frustration. That's when she gave me 'the look'—that gaze that said, 'You need to understand something.'

Sitting me down, my mother revealed that Mrs Newton had once been an active member of our church and a vibrant part of the community. However, her life took a devastating turn when her husband and son were killed in a car accident caused by a drunk driver.

After this heart-wrenching loss, Mrs Newton withdrew from the world, seldom leaving her home. 'Her whole world crumbled and she couldn't face it. That's why she asks you for help; she's terribly lonely,' my mom explained.

Learning about this tragedy changed my perspective. I began to appreciate the enormity of her loss and the pain she must have been enduring.

One day, I mustered the courage to tell her that my mother had shared the story of her family's tragic fate. I expressed my sympathy for her loss, and in response, Mrs Newton burst into tears. I felt utterly helpless, not knowing how to console her. She gestured for me to leave, and I did as she requested.

For the following three weeks, I continued to make attempts to collect her subscription, but she did not answer the door. I knew she was inside, but she remained unresponsive. I couldn't help but feel a deep sense of guilt.

Finally, nearly a month later, the door cracked open, and she invited me inside. This time, instead of asking for help, she gestured for me to sit in a chair. Over the next half-hour, she poured out her heart, sharing stories about her son, her husband, her life, and more. Though she cried throughout our conversation, she managed to speak without interruption.

As she concluded her emotional narrative, she reached out and placed her hand on my arm. She said, 'I've been carrying this pain for so long, and nobody wants to visit me because I'm always so sad.

I realize this now. I need to move forward; I just don't know how. Thank you for listening.'

Overwhelmed by the experience, I promptly relayed the story to my mother, who also teared up. Without hesitation, she picked up the phone and reached out to several of Mrs Newton's neighbours. She implored them to visit and offer their support.

Over time, Mrs Newton's life began to transform. She started tending to her yard, taking leisurely walks along Mountain Road, and even returned to our church. She underwent a remarkable change.

Sometimes, people don't know how to reach out for help, and it's up to us to extend a helping hand. We must be there for each other, even when it's not immediately evident that someone is in need.

How to Spend Time with a Workaholic Father

What can I possibly say about my father? He was undeniably a workaholic, devoted to his profession with an unwavering dedication that shaped his daily routine. Each morning, like clockwork, he would rise at 5.30 a.m. and prepare himself for the day ahead. By 6.15 a.m., he would leave for work, and although he would return home punctually at 5.30 p.m., his work did not end there. After dinner, he would immerse himself once more, toiling diligently into the late hours.

My father, a brilliant and renowned meteorologist, had revolutionized the field by transforming the insurance industry's ability to forecast the impact of natural disasters. His work was truly remarkable and had left an indelible mark on his profession. However, due to his relentless work habits, my five siblings and I had limited opportunities to bask in his presence. Yet, there was one exception to this rule—an exception we cherished dearly—badminton.

While badminton may not have been my personal passion, we all recognized the sheer joy it brought to our father, and we would seize any chance to entice him into playing.

Armed with a badminton racket, I would venture into his workspace after dinner, playfully taunting, 'Father, are you ready to lose once again? You are getting old and slow. We are all warmed up. Or are you afraid? I think you are afraid. That must be it.'

He would pause and contemplate the demands on his time. Then he would rise from his seat, grasp the racket, and assert, 'I have fifteen minutes.' And yet, those fifteen minutes would invariably stretch into an hour of spirited play.

Across our front lawn was a wooden fence that served as the perfect court for our game. What astounded me about my father was his natural finesse—his ability to return every shot effortlessly, seemingly without exerting much effort himself.

For those of us who had fathers consumed by their work, finding avenues of connection became imperative. Badminton became my way of engaging with my father, bridging the gap between his demanding profession and our need for his presence.

As I embarked on my own journey of fatherhood, I carried forward the tradition, spending countless hours on the badminton court with my own children. When they were young, I would deliberately let them taste victory more often than not, fostering their enthusiasm for the game. However, as they grew older, I found myself evolving into a seasoned player, unleashing shots from every corner of the court with little effort.

Damien, my youngest, emerged as the true champion, surpassing my skills over time. The pride I feel for him knows no bounds.

Both my father and mother have since departed this world. For those who have experienced the loss of their parents, a feeling of orphanhood often lingers. I, too, find myself grappling with this sentiment, forever missing their presence, their warmth, their unwavering love. The void they left in my heart endures.

When these feelings surface, I simply recall our epic badminton games, along with the amazing childhood experiences brought about by my loving parents. This always brings a smile to my face.

* * *

Looking back, it is clear that my journey into the fight against modern slavery did not follow a predetermined path. In fact, during my youth, I had no inkling that I would engage with any cause of significance. But I can see in these stories the beginning of many threads in the tapestry of my life.

As a shy and introverted individual, I was often attuned to the struggles of others, quietly observing the injustices of the world around me. This sensitivity and desire for fairness laid the groundwork for my later advocacy.

Furthermore, the small-town environment in which I grew up instilled in me a sense of community and collective responsibility. Its close-knit nature fostered my desire to help others and make a positive impact.

There may be no direct line connecting my childhood experiences to my later career, but I have no doubt the culmination of these early influences shaped my values, passions, and sense of purpose.

Thus, my journey from timid boy to global activist is testament not only to the power of childhood experiences, but to how seemingly ordinary events can shape our lives and transform us into agents of change.

7

Lessons from My Teenage Years

Adolescence is a critical link between childhood and adulthood, characterized by major physical, psychological, and social transitions. When I look back at my teenage years, I realize that many of my most memorable experiences involved moments of personal failure and inadequacy that influenced my thoughts, emotions, and feelings about things. It was not a great time in my life.

The events below—both the positive and the negative ones—have influenced and shaped the person I am, and the one I will become.

Every Embarrassing Detail there in Print

During my formative teenage years, my mother wrote a weekly column for our local newspaper. Titled 'Footprints, Heartbeat & Dreams'; it served as an outlet for her thoughts, weaving together 500 words of opinion, fairy tales, and amusing anecdotes. Often, she would recount the comical and occasionally mortifying adventures and mishaps involving herself and her brood of six children, me included.

Being one of those kids who liked to push the boundaries of what life had to offer, I frequently found myself caught in peculiar and awkward situations. To my dismay, if my mother caught wind of these escapades, they would invariably find their way into her column, where the most intimate details of my life would be laid bare for all to see, including my high-school classmates.

In her writings, she often lovingly referred to me as her 'nature boy.' I recall one instance where she chronicled the time I went fishing, only to have the hook become entangled in my own ear following a misguided cast. Imagine how embarrassing this was for a teenager just trying to fit in.

These stories were not limited to mere anecdotes. They also delved into some of the most cringe-worthy moments of my life. In one case, my mother recounted in excruciating detail one of my disastrous attempts to ask a girl out over the phone. I can still feel the burning humiliation that followed when my peers, armed with my mother's column, approached me with mischievous grins, ready to tease me about the latest tale.

There was little I could say in response. After all, she was my mother. Writing was her passion, and the act of sharing our lives through her column was her way of expressing herself.

Over time, I resigned myself to shrugging off the mortification, realizing that attempting to dissuade her would be an exercise in futility. Once she set her mind on something, nothing could change it. This unwavering determination was one of the qualities I admired most about her, but it also made me apprehensive.

During those tumultuous years of adolescence, marked by awkwardness, acne, insecurity, and a constant sense of uncertainty, the last thing I desired was a glaring spotlight on my goofy and mortifying journey through this challenging phase of life. I yearned for privacy, seeking solace in the notion that my teenage follies would eventually fade into distant memories.

Yet, as I reflect upon those times now, I find myself without regret. In fact, I have come to appreciate what my mother did. When I began writing this book, I could not comprehend why I felt compelled to share these nostalgic tales. Now I understand that it is my personal way of honouring my mother's legacy.

My mother was an extraordinary individual, whose influence extended far beyond the boundaries of her role as a parent.

While she was far from perfect, her love, compassion, kindness, and unwavering pursuit of a fulfilling life were unparalleled. It is for this reason that I dedicate much of my writing to her. It is my heartfelt tribute to a woman who remains eternally loved and deeply missed.

With boundless love and longing, I say, 'I love you and miss you, Mom!'

We Do Not Need Your Advice, Go Away!

One weekend, when I was thirteen years old, I was invited to offer some training at a Boy Scouts outing. Once my responsibilities were fulfilled, I took a leisurely walk along a nearby river. It was during this stroll that a group of four middle-aged men, out in the river fishing, caught my attention. My curiosity piqued, I stopped to watch what they were doing.

These anglers were a sight to behold, adorned with the trappings of their pastime. Their ensemble comprised of top-of-the-line rods, reels gleaming with quality craftsmanship, sturdy high boots, and meticulously packed tackle boxes. Not to mention their attire—matching fishing shirts and pants. To add a touch of whimsy, their hats had lures dangling enticingly from the sides. They certainly looked the part.

As I quietly watched them, it became evident that their preparations, however meticulous, had not yielded any results. Despite their impressive gear and experienced appearance, they were struggling to catch even a single fish. Then it dawned upon me—an idea I couldn't help but share.

As one of the men baited his hook, I approached him and offered a friendly suggestion, 'Perhaps, trying a smaller fishing hook—say, size eight to ten—might lead to more luck catching trout. Their mouths are small. It is much easier to catch them on a small hook.'

The man's eyes locked onto mine, his gaze assessing my youthful countenance, and with a dismissive sneer, he replied, 'Run along, Sonny. We don't need any of your advice. We have everything we need.'

As I walked away, I could hear them laugh. My earnest intention had been misunderstood and unappreciated by these men who saw nothing but a naïve teenager.

Undeterred by their rudeness, I continued along the winding path, eventually stumbling upon a modest clearing beside the flowing river—a stop that appeared to be frequented by many anglers. Inspired by my earlier encounter, I resolved to try my own luck at catching a few fish.

Scanning the shoreline, I discovered a discarded jumble of tangled fishing line and painstakingly untangled it, eventually salvaging a useful fifteen feet. I then scoured the vicinity, eventually spotting a protruding log from the water, to which an abandoned fishing hook clung stubbornly. Turning over several rocks, I unearthed a collection of squirming worms—an ideal bait for my impromptu fishing expedition. During similar solitary walks, I had become a seasoned hand at finding the essentials I needed to start fishing, even when I came without any bait or tackle.

With my hook baited and my line cast beneath a tranquil, shaded spot, I waited. To my delight, within a mere fifteen minutes, my patience bore fruit—a medium-sized trout took my bait. Encouraged by this initial triumph, I repeated the process, pulling in three more fish.

Realizing I needed to get back, I made my way down the path to where the scouting event was taking place, the four prized trout dangling gracefully by my side. As I nonchalantly passed by the very men who had dismissed me earlier, they all turned to take in my impressive catch.

One of them, clearly taken aback, inquired, 'Where did you get those fish?'

'I caught them down the river,' I replied with a hint of mischief in my tone.

His curiosity growing, he asked, 'But how? I don't see any fishing pole or equipment with you.'

Emboldened, and with a modest smile, I said, 'I found what I needed and simply caught them. Fishing is remarkably simple.

You just need to know what you are doing. Have you managed to catch any yet?'

They stared at me, their mouths agape. No other words were exchanged, only a lingering silence and a sense of reflection. And so, I continued my journey, leaving them to contemplate the lessons that had unfolded before their eyes.

From an early age, I had discovered that wisdom knows no age limits; that insights can come from the unlikeliest sources. We all possess the capacity to learn from one another, but only if we keep an open mind.

He Raised His Fist and Waved It in Front of Me

From a young age, my proficiency in the Boy Scouts propelled me through the ranks at an impressive pace. By the time I turned thirteen, I had already ascended to the rank of 'Star' and was entrusted with leading my own patrol, a responsibility largely attributed to my mother's influence. However, despite my rapid progression, I often found myself lacking the maturity to fully embrace my role. Nevertheless, due to my rank, I was perceived as more advanced than my fellow scouts.

One summer, we received an invitation to attend a Boy Scouts Jamboree, a gathering where scouts from across the state converged for joint activities, competitions, and networking sessions. After being assigned a location, my patrol, consisting of five scruffy kids, including myself, set about the challenge of pitching our tents. As usual, this proved quite daunting, exacerbating the 'imposter syndrome' that frequently plagued me.

The first day of the jamboree was exhilarating. We engaged in spirited games of 'capture the flag', honed our archery skills, and in the evening attended a grand bonfire. However, upon returning to our campsite we were confronted with the unwelcome presence of another, older group of scouts who had set up their tents beside us. That night, our neighbours indulged in heavy drinking, and to our dismay, one of them ventured over to our site and defiled one of our tents by urinating on it. Their unruly behaviour left us all in a state of fear.

The following morning, as my patrol made its way towards the dining hall for breakfast, we were intercepted by three adult leaders. They asked who the patrol leader was, and I hesitantly raised my hand. One of the men spoke up, 'We received complaints about the boys camping next to you who were drinking. We are heading there now. Can you tell us what you saw?'

Silence and apprehension gripped me. I understood that if these boys found out we tattled on them, it might result in some kind of retaliation. However, my patrol members, undeterred by my silence, proceeded to offer every graphic detail to the concerned leaders. Their accounts were damning.

After breakfast, we returned to our campsite, only to find the boys in question and their tents conspicuously absent. Relief washed over me. Unfortunately, it was short-lived. Out of nowhere, those same boys barged into our camp, their presence imposing and threatening.

One of them singled us out and demanded, 'Who is the leader here?' In unison, my patrol members pointed at me. Though I hadn't uttered a word, I knew there was no point in clarifying that fact.

Summoning whatever courage I could muster, I tremulously declared, 'I am the patrol leader.'

'You ratted us out to the organizers, and now we're in big trouble. It's time for you to pay,' one of them sneered, raising his fist in a menacing display. His knuckles whitened as he clenched his hand, poised to strike me across the face. I didn't flinch, not because I was brave, but because I was too frightened to move.

'What should we do with you?' he menacingly inquired; his intent palpable.

With a shaky voice, I managed to stammer, 'I suggest you leave. Trust me, you don't want any further trouble with the adults. If you hit me, there will be legal consequences. Your parents will be brought into this. You don't want that. Just leave.'

A prolonged pause ensued as he deliberated my words. Then, without warning, he pushed me to the ground, turned on his heel and departed, the others reluctantly following suit.

As soon as they disappeared, my body succumbed to the fear that had gripped me. Hyperventilation took hold, leaving me gasping for breath and teetering on the brink of losing consciousness.

That incident has remained in my memory ever since. In many ways, it helped to prepare me for those times when as an adult I would face genuine peril. I came to comprehend the harsh reality of violence, its capacity to strike without warning. Understanding how to navigate such situations and choosing the right words and actions became imperative for my personal growth and safety later in life.

What Have I Done? Yikes!

It was Thanksgiving evening, and I found myself in the company of my three best friends: Doug, Scott, and Neil. As thirteen-year-olds, we often struggled to find excitement during the late hours of the night, so we aimlessly strolled through our town, hoping for something to ignite our sense of adventure. Eventually, we stumbled upon a local school, and a peculiar idea sparked in my mind.

Looking up at the entrance, a realization struck me: the positioning of the building allowed for a potential climb to the roof. Craving an adrenaline rush and yearning for something interesting to do, I decided to scale the structure. Persuading Scott and Doug to join me, we left Neil behind as we ascended.

Once on the rooftop, a surge of adrenaline coursed through our veins as we sprinted along its length and back again. Our hearts pounding, we felt a rush like never before. However, as we prepared to descend, a chilling sight awaited us below: five police cars and a dozen officers armed with flashlights, scouring the grounds.

Despite the shock, we remained composed and made our way down. Approaching one of the officers, we nervously inquired, 'Are you searching for us?' They hadn't noticed our rooftop escapade.

Unexpectedly, the three of us were whisked away, taken in separate police cars to the local station. Isolated in individual rooms, the gravity of the situation sank in as I gazed upon the stern countenance of the officer in charge.

'How did you break into the school? Our sensors detected your presence in the hallway,' he interrogated, his expression unyielding.

Tears streaming down my cheeks, I pleaded, 'We never entered the school. We merely climbed to the roof. It was my idea, and we meant no harm. We just ran to the end and returned. We were up there only for a short time.'

After the officer explained that our parents were on their way, he departed, leaving me alone in that stark room. In that moment, it felt as if my world was crumbling around me. Questions swirled in my mind: What would my parents say? Would this tarnish my record? What had I done?

This incident was a pivotal moment in my life because it thrust me into my first major crisis. The consequences of a decision I had made rippled far beyond anything I had done previously.

When my parents arrived, their disappointment was palpable, yet their anger remained mild. However, I was compelled to accept responsibility for my actions by personally calling the other parents. Although no charges were pressed against us, the night still resonates with me due to the unkind and hurtful names hurled at me by those adults. It was an undeniably traumatic experience.

Reflecting upon this event, I now understand that our actions were relatively harmless, but at the time, they felt monumental. It seemed like the world was ending. It is remarkable how certain life experiences can amplify our emotions.

That day taught me one thing: breaking the rules can have grave and unforeseen consequences. It showed me the importance of understanding the effects that our choices have and of taking responsibility when we err. It also taught me to channel my natural restlessness and desire to explore towards more constructive endeavours.

I Was Out of Control, about to Crash

When I was fourteen, I impulsively enrolled in a class on how to take apart and then put together small lawnmower engines. Initially, I expected to loathe the class, but to my surprise, I grew to love it. The sensation of getting my hands dirty with grease and grime was oddly satisfying, and there was a certain masculinity that accompanied the process of breaking down and resurrecting an engine. Once the class concluded, I was determined to apply my new-found skills. That's when the idea of building a go-cart struck me.

I scoured the local classifieds and stumbled upon an ad for a go-cart frame. It had succumbed to rust and required refurbishment, so I was able to buy it for a mere $15. Bringing it home, I painstakingly sanded it down and painted it a vibrant shade of orange. Next, I procured used tyres, a clutch, and a chain. To power this magnificent creation, I bought a disabled snowblower. While the engine was bigger than I needed, it served its purpose flawlessly. With the help of my friends, we took it apart, repurposed it, and mounted it onto the frame. The entire investment for this extraordinary Frankenstein-like machine amounted to a mere $50.

Yet, as I revelled in the excitement of my creation, there were two crucial aspects I hadn't fully thought out—the foot throttle and brakes. Anxious to experience the go-cart's potential, I improvised a rudimentary set-up using a string and a rubber band to serve as a makeshift throttle control, with the rubber band retracting it to idle. The plan was simple: venture up the street, make a turn, and come back to assess its performance.

As the engine roared to life, I embarked on this exhilarating journey. The sheer thrill of driving the go-cart was beyond measure. Within seconds, I found myself hurtling up the road at a breathtaking speed. Realizing that I could decelerate simply by releasing the throttle, I made the decision to turn right onto Brentwood Road. To conquer the uphill stretch, I applied a generous amount of gas.

However, as the road began its descent, disaster struck. The rubber band snapped with the engine still at full throttle. With no brakes to rely on, I was thrust into a terrifying predicament. Fear surged through me as I hurtled down the road, desperately searching for a means to regain control. Miraculously, I managed to execute a hair-raising right-turn onto my street, barely managing to balance on two wheels.

As I zoomed past my house, the neighbourhood kids erupted into cheers, unaware of the danger I was in.

'Help! I can't stop this thing! I have no brakes! I'm in trouble!' I shouted. Alas, my words were drowned out by their cheers as I whizzed by at a mind-boggling speed of 40 miles per hour.

Realizing the potential for serious injury, I made a split-second decision. Summoning all my courage, I accelerated up the steep hill, guiding the go-cart to the edge of Cedar Mountain, up a dusty trail, and finally crashing it into a cluster of small trees. While this manoeuvre helped me come to a stop without harm, it came at a heavy price—the front end of my beloved creation was seriously damaged.

A few minutes later, the others arrived, perplexed by my decision to crash my glorious creation. They failed to comprehend the grave danger I had faced, unable to fathom the risks that had threatened my life.

Today, I often find myself pondering the lessons of that perilous day. I had taken risks that could have proven fatal yet, paradoxically, those same risks were to save my life on numerous occasions in the years to come because they taught me the need for prudence and caution in the face of danger.

I Have Been Bitten by over 100 Snakes

During a recent podcast interview, I was asked to share an aspect of my life that set me apart from most others. Without hesitation, I proudly revealed I had been bitten by over 100 snakes. Naturally, the host was taken aback.

Many people find snakes intimidating. Roughly 33 per cent of the global population suffers from ophidiophobia, the fear of snakes, making it the second most common phobia worldwide after fear of death. However, I have always held a deep appreciation for these magnificent creatures.

My journey with snakes began when I was just five years old. Exploring the fields near my childhood home, I would fearlessly approach any non-poisonous snake I could find. Although some would instinctively nip at me when I tried to handle them, their bites never bothered me. After all, it's in a snake's nature to bite when picked up, and their bites were far from painful.

While I kept numerous snakes as pets over the years, my first substantial companion was a six-foot boa constrictor. I acquired this majestic creature during a visit to a port in New York City, where, occasionally, serpents would hitch a ride on cargo ships carrying fruits and vegetables. Ports don't usually know what to do with these unexpected passengers, so they often sell them to pet shops. On that day, luck was on my side. I managed to buy a boa for a bargain $25.

Wearing my reptilian friend like an exotic accessory, I would often stroll around town with the snake coiled comfortably around my neck. The reactions of the small suburban community of Newington never failed to amuse me. It was during these moments that I became acutely aware of the widespread fear people held towards snakes.

One incident involved my sister's boyfriend, Burt, a rugged and self-assured individual who exuded an aura of control in every aspect of his life. However, whenever I entered a room accompanied by a snake, Burt would leap onto the nearest couch and emit a high-pitched scream, his fear exposing a primal vulnerability.

I also recall the time my beloved snake managed to escape from its wooden enclosure in our basement. For half a year, we scoured the house desperately searching for our missing reptile, much to the dismay of my three older sisters. Then, one day, I went into the basement and there he was, emerging gracefully from a hole in the wall. With a sense of relief, I gently returned him to his wooden abode and nourished him.

Eventually, for reasons I cannot precisely recall, I decided to part ways with my pet boa constrictor. Little did I know that this would not mark the end of my encounters with these legless marvels.

During a visit to Brazil, I was presented with the remarkable opportunity to hold a 250-pound, 15-foot anaconda. This snake had sustained injuries in the Brazilian jungle and was under care and treatment. While handling such a powerful creature posed a risk, I managed to prevent any unwanted bites or mishaps.

Throughout the years, I have helped many individuals conquer their deep-seated fear of snakes. The process involves a fundamental shift in mindset and requires determination on behalf of the 'patient' to reprogramme their mind. Gradually, the person progresses from looking at a snake and being near one, to tentatively touching it under supervision, and finally to holding one all by themselves. At the end of the process, if it has been successful, the person will have a newfound sense of empowerment.

I've found this approach works not only with our fear of snakes, but with all the fears we encounter in life.

Through empathy, understanding, and a willingness to confront our phobias head-on, we can forge deep connections with the natural world and ultimately conquer the fears that hold us back.

I Finally Gave In to the Peer Pressure

During my freshman year of high school, I had a brilliant idea. Instead of using a regular backpack to lug my books back and forth, I opted for something a little out of the ordinary—a hard-shell briefcase I stumbled upon at a tag sale. Little did I know that this decision would attract quite a lot of attention.

From the moment I stepped foot into the school grounds, eyes turned in my direction. People glanced at my face, then shifted their gaze to the briefcase, and finally, back to me again. Back then, such a departure from the norm was simply unheard of.

Soon enough, the questions started pouring in from my curious friends. They couldn't help but ask, 'What's the deal with that thing you're carrying around? Isn't it a bit odd for school?' I chuckled and replied, 'Hey, it's practical. Everything I need fits in here perfectly.' Their puzzled expressions were usually followed by another query, 'But aren't you worried about what people will think of you and your choice?'

My response was, 'Who cares?'

Nevertheless, the inquiries kept coming, and older students felt the need to voice their opinions too. 'What's up with you? Are you some kind of freak?' they asked, or, 'Look at the little businessman. Are you off to sell something?' The most outrageous comment came from a particularly bold classmate who quipped, 'Only an alien would walk around with something like that. Are you from outer space?' Each time, I laughed off these remarks. I firmly believed it was my life, my choice, and nobody had the right to dictate otherwise.

For nearly a month, I proudly carried on with my briefcase crusade, determined not to let societal norms stifle my individuality. It became a matter of principle for me. However, high school can be an unforgiving environment when it comes to straying from the pack. The more I resisted conformity, the greater the peer pressure became.

My friends began to distance themselves from me as the personal attacks escalated. I was shunned. Instead of simply accepting me as the 'kid with the weird briefcase', the consensus seemed to be that I needed to be brought back in line with the rest of them.

Like many others who dared to be different, I eventually succumbed to defeat. Swimming against the tide became increasingly difficult once I lost the support of my closest friends. I discovered that only a few individuals in the herd stood by me. It was a painful lesson to learn.

Reflecting on those times, I wonder if things have changed in schools today. This happened a long time ago, and I'm uncertain of the current climate. Sometimes, I wonder if I should have persevered and continued carrying my beloved briefcase. But deep down, I understood that I lacked the strength to face down the relentless pressure and bullying. Peer influence can be an immense personal constraint, stifling creativity, individuality, and personal independence.

Although it took me much of my young adult life to outgrow my concerns about others' opinions, I eventually reached a point where I no longer cared. I only wish I had attained this liberating mindset at the tender age of fourteen. Just imagine where I would be today.

Our clubhouse

When I was fifteen years old, my closest friends—Scott, Doug, and Neil—were always on the lookout for a place where we could hang out together, away from the prying eyes and noise of our respective homes. Unfortunately, our options were limited, as privacy was a rare luxury with parents and siblings around. But fate had something unexpected in store for us.

One sunny afternoon, while strolling down Connecticut Avenue, our eyes fell upon an old AMC Rambler car languishing in the backyard of a neighbour's house. Its dilapidated appearance suggested it had been there for ages, with faded paint, rust eating away at its body, and even plants sprouting from the engine bay. Two flat tyres completed the sad picture.

Seizing the opportunity, the four of us approached the owner, mustering up the courage to ask if he would consider parting ways with the forlorn vehicle. To our surprise, he agreed to sell it to us for just $30, on the condition that we remove it from his property. We gathered our resources, pooling our meagre savings, and triumphantly acquired this beast of a car.

With sheer determination, we managed to push the Rambler to the home of a generous family friend who kindly allowed us to park it under a sprawling tree on the edge of his yard. The transformation had begun. This rusted relic was to become our labour of love.

Despite our limited knowledge of mechanics, we dove into the task of resurrecting the old motor. The car was an utter mess, its engine barely recognizable beneath layers of rust. But with perseverance and countless hours of tinkering, we eventually coaxed it back to life.

That battered car became our haven, our very own clubhouse. Over the course of two memorable years, we congregated within its battered shell, escaping the world's pressures, and losing ourselves in camaraderie. It was a place where we shared meals, engaged in lively discussions, and listened to music that spoke to our souls. Every teenage rite of passage played out within those worn seats—cars, motorcycles, school, sports, politics, girls, and, of course, matters of the heart.

While some might dismiss the old, decrepit vehicle as an eyesore, for us, it was a sanctuary amidst the chaos of adolescence. It represented a physical space we collectively owned, free from the influence of parents or external forces. It was our own personal refuge—a small patch of real estate where we forged bonds that would last a lifetime.

But something unexpected happened. One day, as we approached the spot where our refuge stood, our hearts sank. It was gone. Vanished without a trace. We turned to the house owner, hoping for answers, but he was as clueless as we were.

What could have happened to our beloved preserve? Had a disgruntled neighbour orchestrated its removal due to its unsightliness? Had someone brazenly stolen it away under the cover of night? Or perhaps the town authorities had deemed it a hazard and disposed of it. It was a riddle, wrapped in a mystery, inside the enigma of the car's two flat tyres.

The loss was a devastating blow to us all. Our treasured clubhouse, the very heart of our adolescent adventures, had vanished into thin air. An emptiness settled in our hearts and minds, a void that could never be filled. The memories created within those four weathered doors would remain forever in our souls, a testament to a time when that old Rambler was our sanctuary, and the world, our oyster.

This experience reflected the transformative power of friendship, the significance of personal spaces in shaping memories, and the enduring impact of shared experiences during this pivotal period in life.

Matt, Are You Really Smart Enough to Attend College?

When I began my junior year of high school, I found myself obligated to meet with the school guidance counsellor several times to discuss my future. In our initial encounter, I couldn't shake the feeling that this middle-aged man didn't like me.

Our first meeting lasted a mere twenty minutes. He urged me to think about my future and scheduled a follow-up appointment at the beginning of the upcoming year.

As our second meeting commenced, he skimmed through a file labelled with my name and asked, 'Have you given any thought to your future?'

I responded confidently, 'I plan on attending college.'

To my surprise, his smile faded. 'You should also consider other options, like trade school or finding a job,' he said.

I couldn't understand why he did not encourage my pursuit of a college education. So I asked why he had recommended trade school.

'Well, your grades aren't exceptional. College can be challenging, and not everyone succeeds. It is my job to prepare you for the realities of life, which can sometimes be harsh. Why subject yourself to the potential failure of dropping out of college?' he asked.

He continued to elaborate on why college might not be the right fit for me, highlighting my strengths in car repair and shop courses. He tried to persuade me that a career in the trades could provide a decent salary and be my true calling in life.

His words disheartened me.

Throughout high school, I had many discussions with teachers, coaches, and other mentors, but this particular one haunted me. It pained me to hear an authority figure pass judgment on my abilities and suggest that I lacked the intelligence and potential for self-improvement.

Although I had an inkling that I would prove him wrong, his words continued to affect me for the next decade. Whenever faced with difficulties during my college journey, his words resurfaced, echoing, 'Why subject yourself to the misery of attempting college?'

For years, I grappled with imposter syndrome, even though I excelled in college and early job experiences. I constantly looked over my shoulder, fearing that everyone around me would suddenly realize I wasn't as intelligent as I appeared.

One day, after returning home following a United Nations field visit eight years after my high school graduation, I shared the story of this discouraging encounter with my parents. At this time, I was twenty-six years old. They simply laughed.

'Are you kidding me? Did you believe him?' my mom exclaimed. 'You have an incredible mind. You have the capability to achieve anything you set your mind to. Don't you understand that?'

My encounter with this guidance counsellor showed me how great an influence authority figures hold over the self-worth and self-perception of the young. I had unwittingly embraced his pessimistic snap judgments about my character, based solely on his brief perusal of my grades. He knew nothing about me.

In hindsight though, I am grateful to the counsellor. He inadvertently provided my primary motivation to uplift and empower the many young people I encounter. It was my antidote to his 'guidance.'

Why Do You Always Shout at Me?

When I was sixteen years old, I decided to join the high school swim team. Looking back, I'm not entirely sure why. While swimming had been a part of my life since the age of two, I was never known for my speed in the water. No matter how hard I tried, my best efforts never earned me more than a fourth-place finish in any of my races.

What made my decision even more perplexing was that it often felt like Coach Hall harboured some sort of disdain for me. Almost every practice, I found myself singled out, subjected to his critical remarks. 'Friedman, you're not pulling your weight,' he would yell. 'You're not working hard enough. Do another six laps. Don't be such a slacker.'

Oddly enough, he would then turn to another swimmer, perhaps Jacobs, and offer words of encouragement. 'Good job out there, Jacobs. Keep working on your stroke.'

I couldn't understand why Coach Hall seemed to consistently target me while sparing others. It ignited a burning anger within me, driving me to seek some answers. Determined but apprehensive, I approached Coach Hall after one of our gruelling practices, nervously entering his office.

I stammered, 'I don't understand why you're so hard on me. I'm trying my best. Jacobs and I swim the same number of laps, yet you shout at me and say nothing to him. I don't understand why you treat me differently.'

For what felt like an eternity, Coach Hall regarded me with a pensive gaze. Finally, breaking the silence, he offered a half-smile and began to speak. 'When you first joined the team, you were an average swimmer,' he acknowledged. 'But over time, you've improved significantly. I'm genuinely proud of your achievements. However, I believe you're capable of even greater things.'

Stunned, I remained silent, unsure of how to react to this unexpected glimmer of positivity. I waited, curious to hear what he had to say next.

'Jacobs is a sensitive boy,' Coach Hall continued. 'If I were to raise my voice at him, he would shut down. He thrives on my encouragement. That's why I provide it. But you are different. When I challenge you, you rise to the occasion. You seem determined to prove me wrong, and that fiery determination pushes you to give a staggering 120 per cent of your effort. When you first started, you were frequently defeated, but now you stand as a formidable contender.'

Coach Hall paused, allowing his words to sink in. I was speechless.

'I don't say these things to be mean to you,' Coach Hall reassured. 'I genuinely believe you can do better. I apologize if my approach has upset you. If you prefer, I can stop pushing you. But deep down, I don't believe that's what you need. It may appear as though I single you out, but I offer similar challenges to most of the boys. It's just that you focus solely on what is said to you.'

He was right. I had undeniably improved, and it was in those moments of challenging criticism that I found the strength to push myself further. It seemed to be precisely what I required to grow.

Years later, I came to understand that many of my most valuable lessons came from mentors, teachers, and coaches who truly understood what it took to inspire and motivate me—even when it wasn't pleasant to hear.

She Came to My Rescue

When I turned sixteen, I took a job at a burger café to fund my college education and spent the next two years of high school putting in a thirty-five-hour workweek on top of my academic work. On Friday nights, my shift stretched from 3.30 p.m. to 3.30 a.m.

One evening, a remarkable woman by the name of Mrs Kellogg came to the restaurant for a meal with her friends. Mrs Kellogg had always been an imposing figure in our town. She held sway on various town committees, championed fundraising efforts for important town projects, and commanded the respect and admiration of all who knew her. Her family's name adorned several schools and other public landmarks, a testament to their enduring legacy.

As her friends settled down at a table, Mrs Kellogg welcomed me with a warm smile and kind words about the volunteer projects I had undertaken as a Boy Scouts. Her ability to uplift and honour those around her was truly remarkable.

However, the tranquillity was soon disrupted as another group entered the restaurant: 'Mean girls' from the local high school accompanied by their boyfriends.

While I generally took pride in my work, I braced myself for trouble whenever this particular group appeared. As I approached their table to take their orders, the onslaught began.

'Matt, you're still here, working away. Do you even have a life? Friends, perhaps?' one of them sneered.

I remained silent, doing my best to efficiently handle their orders. But the insults and jabs persisted.

'I must say, Matt, that uniform suits you splendidly. Maybe you should wear it to school. It's your colour,' they taunted, laughing at their own comments.

Throughout their stay, they sent dishes back, made frivolous requests, and did everything in their power to provoke me. Despite the mounting anger within me, I kept my composure. In the service industry, one is often left with no choice but to endure such behaviour; it is part of the job.

Just as their abuse seemed to reach its zenith, Mrs Kellogg made her way over to their table. She greeted each of them by name, a warm smile on her face.

'Hello, Kelly. How's your evening going? Always a pleasure to see you. How's your mother? I'll be meeting with her tomorrow. And Ricky, that catch at the football game last week was truly impressive. It's wonderful to see all of you tonight.' She addressed each person with genuine warmth.

'Oh, Matt,' she said, turning her attention to me, 'could you please bring me the bill? That burger was absolutely fantastic. And could you drop by my office at the Town Hall sometime next week? After school, perhaps? I'd like you to meet the mayor; he's quite interested in your recycling initiatives. I also have a few ideas to expand your already remarkable proposals. I'm thoroughly impressed.'

'Of course, Mrs Kellogg,' I replied, taken aback by her unexpected offer.

She concluded with a wink, 'Please convey my regards to your mother; I truly appreciate all that you both do.'

And with that, she left a tip that was double the usual amount.

From that day forward, that troublesome group kept their distance from me. Mrs Kellogg's endorsement served as a clear message to them: 'Stay away from this young man—he's someone I wholeheartedly support—or else!'

On that memorable day, she came to my rescue, and I couldn't have been more grateful for the outcome.

* * *

During adolescence, I had many experiences of personal failure and inadequacy that left lasting impressions on me. But when I reflect on the ups and downs of those years, I can see they helped shape my commitment to fighting human trafficking.

My own struggles helped me to develop the empathy I needed to understand the vulnerability, pain, and challenges faced by those who have been trafficked. They also fired within me a deep sense of responsibility, that I must fight for a world free from exploitation.

As I formed friendships, navigated peer pressure and became more aware of inequality and other societal issues, I found I couldn't ignore injustice and suffering in the world. It inspired me to use my voice to create change for those who couldn't find a voice of their own.

The teenage years are a time of transitions. My body underwent dramatic changes as I went through puberty, which influenced my self-image and confidence. Accepting and understanding these changes taught me to be resilient and strive to overcome obstacles, qualities that have proven invaluable later in life.

Finally, psychologically, adolescence is a period of intense self-discovery. I often found myself questioning my values, beliefs, and purpose in life. Doing so gave me a clearer understanding of my strengths, weaknesses, and passions, which in turn gave me the insight to pursue a career aligned with my convictions.

8

Adult Milestones

I have encountered many lessons over the years that have shaped my journey. But these lessons did not end in childhood. The learning process is ongoing; to this day, I continue to grow and evolve. Even as an adult, it is important to learn from both positive and negative experiences. That is the only way to avoid blindly repeating the mistakes of others.

Here are some of the most pivotal moments from my adult life; those that have shaped my journey and my role as a human trafficking activist.

How a Car Accident Changed the Direction of My Life

It was a crisp morning in 1984 when I found myself humming along in the back of a taxi, traversing the majestic Brooklyn Bridge. Little did I know that this seemingly ordinary day would take an unexpected turn that would alter the course of my life forever.

As fate would have it, my taxi driver abruptly—and inexplicably—swerved from the left lane to the right, causing a catastrophic collision with a stationary car. The impact propelled me backward with force. Then another car hit us from behind and I was sent forward, crushing my face and body against the unforgiving glass partition.

I was momentarily knocked unconscious, unaware of the ensuing turmoil. The driver, an undocumented immigrant, fled the scene, leaving behind a car engulfed in flames. Amidst the disarray, a few brave, compassionate souls rushed to my aid. They pulled me from the wreckage, extinguished the fire, and did their utmost to prevent me from succumbing to shock. An ambulance soon arrived, whisking me away to a nearby hospital, my face and body a canvas of bruises and swelling. The magnitude of the incident left me a wreck, both physically and emotionally.

Given the severity of my facial injuries, which included a broken nose and other significant wounds, I made the difficult decision to temporarily withdraw from my PhD programme at NYU. Days turned into an agonizingly slow healing process, confining me to the solace of my apartment.

During this period of seclusion, a glimmer of hope emerged in an unexpected place. A dear friend and classmate, who happened to work at the United Nations Population Fund (UNFPA), reached out to me. Sensing my predicament, she posed a proposition, 'While you're healing, would you consider writing a background paper on a health programme based in Zambia?'

With little else to occupy my time and a spark of curiosity lit within me, I agreed. After completing the paper, my friend surprised me with an unexpected request, 'I need you to travel to Zambia and serve as a resource for evaluating the programme.'

Startled and overwhelmed by the mere thought of venturing beyond the confines of my familiar Connecticut upbringing, let alone travelling outside the USA, I hesitated. It was ingrained in me that Friedmans simply didn't travel. But my friend's persistence and unwavering belief in my capabilities eventually broke through my resistance. With great reluctance, I embarked on a journey that would challenge my preconceptions and reshape the direction of my life. Acquiring a passport, securing plane tickets, and setting foot in Kenya, Zambia, and Switzerland became my improbable reality.

The moment I stepped onto African soil, a sense of wonder and enchantment enveloped me, captivating my spirit like never before. The vibrant tapestry of sights, sounds, smells, and tastes fascinated all my senses, and I felt an indescribable connection with the people and their plight. It was in that moment that it dawned on me—I had discovered my true calling—international development.

Ever since that transformative experience, I have never looked back. Instead of completing my PhD in Psychology and establishing a comfortable practice in bustling New York City, I dedicated most of my career to serving others in Asia and beyond. My path led me to the fight against human trafficking and to contribute to public health initiatives, humanitarian endeavours, and disaster relief efforts. Over the years, I traversed the globe, setting foot in more than seventy countries and making a meaningful impact in over forty of them with my work.

Reflecting upon my journey, I find myself pondering an alternate reality; one in which that taxi never swerved, where that accident never transpired. Undoubtedly, my life would have taken a vastly different course—one based on familiarity and comfort.

However, when I contemplate the person I have become, the lives I have touched, and the fulfilment I have found, not a single regret stirs within me. I would not change any aspect of my extraordinary life, even if it meant sparing myself the anguish of that dreadful crash. It was the price I had to pay for the life I have lived.

Occasionally, life presents us with unexpected events that have the power to redefine us. In those moments, it is essential to embrace the outcome and remain open to the possibilities that lie ahead. For me, what initially appeared to be one of the worst incidents in my life ultimately unfolded into a collection of remarkable opportunities and unforeseen blessings.

Do I Really Stereotype?

When I was in college, I attended a captivating talk titled 'Human Nature and the Influence of Stereotyping', which had come highly recommended by my sociology professor. The speaker was an elderly man, distinguished by his white hair and a full beard, who made quite an entrance as he rolled out to the front of the class in a wheelchair. Taking his time, he eventually reached the centre of the stage where he was handed a microphone. The audience patiently awaited his words.

With a calm demeanour, he started by stating, 'In my experience, many individuals tend to make assumptions about others based solely on their appearances. These assumptions often revolve around age, sex, or race. Disability can be another factor. How many of you find yourselves guilty of this? I invite you to raise your hand.' Surprisingly, only 20 out of the 200 people present did so.

For the next ten minutes, he delved into the psychological reasons behind this phenomenon. Although the content sounded academic and theoretical, it failed to resonate with me. However, in a sudden twist, without warning or explanation, the speaker rose from his wheelchair and began walking across the stage while continuing his lecture. This unexpected act left the audience, including myself, in a state of astonishment.

But he wasn't finished. A few minutes later, he unveiled his identity, by removing his beard, hat, and grey wig, revealing a middle-aged man full of energy. It was at this moment he addressed us, saying, 'Please disregard the scientific discourse on stereotyping I just presented. That was some serious bullshit. Instead, I invite you to reflect on how many assumptions you made about me based on my wheelchair and perceived age. Once again, how many of you stereotyped me based on my initial appearance. Come on, be honest.'

This time, nearly all hands were raised, including my own, as the speaker had driven his point home. From that moment onward, he abandoned the stage and transformed the lecture into an engaging discussion with the audience. He posed questions such as, 'Can any of you honestly describe what you just experienced? Ladies, do you feel you are treated differently? If so, in what ways?'

Gradually, the participants began to open up, sharing statements such as, 'When you emerged from the wheelchair, I was taken aback. I had low expectations, although I can't explain why.' Another participant admitted, 'Your transformation confused my mind, and I realize that I still harbour stereotypical assumptions.' A powerful realization emerged as someone added, 'I see now. I didn't think I made judgments based on appearances, but it appears I do.'

This lecturer's dynamic approach offered us an opportunity to examine our own biases and stereotyping tendencies in real time. It was a revelation for me to recognize how often I unknowingly attributed certain traits to people based on specific characteristics they possessed.

These insights reminded me of my mother, who frequently spoke about this issue before she passed away. She would say, 'At eighty, people treat me like a child. It's incredibly frustrating. I may be old, but my mind remains as sharp as ever.'

That day, I grasped the value of experiential and immersive education, as it compels us to scrutinize our assumptions and emotional responses based on something real and tangible. It made me realize that we all possess biases, even if we may not consciously acknowledge them. The most effective way to shed light on these biases is to confront them directly. This lecture did just that.

Should I Seek Revenge?

During one of my summer holidays in the early 2000s, I returned home from Thailand to visit my parents. One afternoon, as I walked into a 7-Eleven store, an unexpected sight awaited me behind the counter—it was Jack G. My shock was palpable. It had been over twenty years since our high school graduation, and the memories flooded back.

Jack was one of the most popular guys in our high school class. With his cool car and the prettiest girlfriends, he effortlessly commanded attention. He was always surrounded by his gang of cool kids, and he seemed destined for great success. In contrast, my high school years were marked by awkwardness and acne. I was a band geek, a math enthusiast, and never experienced the sense of belonging I craved. It was far from a great time in my life; in fact, it ranked among my worst.

Back then, I was a nobody in Jack's eyes, except when he occasionally visited the ice cream restaurant where I worked. On those occasions, he would take jabs at me, revelling in my perceived sadness at working on a Saturday night. 'Don't you have any friends?' he would sneer, followed by taunts about my prospects of becoming an assistant manager if I worked hard enough. His friends would join in the laughter, making me the butt of their jokes.

Now, standing before me in that 7-Eleven, Jack was but a shadow of the larger-than-life cool guy and bully he used to be. After gathering a few items, I mustered the courage to approach him at the counter. I asked if he was Jack G., and his blank look revealed that he didn't recognize me.

'Yes,' he responded. 'Who are you?'

'I went to high school with you. My name is Matt Friedman,' I said, hoping to jog his memory.

For a long moment, he stared, visibly surprised. I wondered what had become of him and his once-great potential, and it seemed as if he could read my thoughts.

'Oh, yes, I remember. What are you doing these days?' he finally responded, not knowing what else to say.

'I work for USAID in Thailand, managing development portfolios,' I replied. 'And what about you?'

'As you can see, here I am,' he replied, his voice tinged with embarrassment, looking down.

In a remarkable twist of fate, our roles had reversed. Seeing him standing there, dejected and broken, wearing the same expression I once had when he visited the restaurant, brought back a flood of long-lost memories.

At that moment, part of me yearned to put him down and repay him for all the humiliating things he had said to me. But as I observed him, a wave of sympathy washed over me, and I chose not to inflict any more pain. At many levels, I understood his feelings just then.

Just as I was about to leave, he looked up and asked, 'I hear that Thailand is nice. What's it like living there?'

Surprised by his genuine interest, I stayed and chatted with him for the next half hour. It turned out that beneath his former façade of popularity and arrogance, he was just a nice, simple guy. By the end of our conversation, all the resentment and unforgiveness that had resurfaced upon seeing him had disappeared.

I realized that seeking revenge and dwelling on past grievances only squanders precious energy that could be better used to create an amazing life. It was best to let go of the people who had wronged me, to forgive them, and instead focus on myself and the ones I love.

An Old Clock Brings a Timely Reminder

During one of my presentation tours in Canada, I was gripped by an insatiable craving for pasta. Unfortunately, my hotel café didn't have what I was looking for, so I searched on the internet for the nearest grocery store and found one a few kilometres away.

As I was making my way there, I noticed a signboard with the words 'Estate Sale' and couldn't resist taking a look.

I arrived at an aged, grand house where a flurry of people were shuffling in and out.

Inside, a vast assortment of once-cherished belongings was strewn across tables and chairs. Household goods, petite collectibles, books, and jewellery all lay in silent testimony to a life well-lived.

The former owner of this treasure trove appeared to have been a world traveller, her mementos from every corner of the globe painting vivid tales of her adventures.

Despite my initial resolve not to buy anything, I stumbled upon a small, antiquated brass alarm clock; its face inscribed with the word 'blessing'. I cradled it in my hand; it had a price tag of just $8. This clock, I decided, must be mine.

Moments later, I found a weathered tome—a collection of the world's beloved poetry for a mere dollar. Poetry had never been my forte, but I was inexplicably drawn towards it. I discovered the book was published in 1894, with a handwritten name inside the cover.

As I made my way to the checkout with these new-found treasures, a framed photograph of an elderly woman caught my eye. Inquiring about the photo, the estate manager informed me that this was Mary, the former occupant of the house, captured in her nineties. Her smile, immortalized in the image, radiated a love for life.

Staring at her photograph, it struck me as strange that so many of us were parcelling out the remnants of what had once been a vital part of Mary's life, me included. A twinge of sadness crept over me as I thought about this notion.

Mary had indeed lived a fulfilling life, but now she was gone, and her cherished collection was scattering like leaves in the wind. For a moment, I felt a wave of sentimentality and nostalgia wash over me. It dawned on me that we are all here for a while, and then we depart, leaving behind fragments of our existence for others to sift through.

Someday, the same will undoubtedly happen to me. My assortment of trinkets will pass into the hands of others, continuing the rhythm of life's eternal dance.

In honour of the clock's inscription, 'blessing', I christened it 'Mary's Blessing'. Whenever I now gaze upon it resting on my shelf, I am reminded of this enigmatic stranger—a small gesture to preserve her memory.

Years after I bought it, as I was penning these very reflections in fact, I randomly flipped open the poetry book to page 80, revealing a verse from Longfellow: 'An ancient timepiece says to all,— / "Forever — never! / Never — forever!"'

It felt like a fitting conclusion. A reminder that we are born, we live, and eventually, we pass on. It's all part of life's cyclical tapestry.

I will never forget standing in Mary's home, sensing that her life had completed its circle. Someday, mine will too.

How Am I Going to Get Out of This Terrible Mess?

Years ago, I found myself in a seemingly impossible situation while driving my old Toyota station wagon along a remote road in Nepal.

The car had a history of overheating, and just as luck would have it, it stalled as I rounded a corner.

Concerned about the possibility of being hit by a passing bus, I managed to steer the vehicle over to the side of the road, hoping it would cool down. However, in my distracted state, I failed to notice the deep ditch in front of me. My front tyre plunged into the pit, leaving my car stuck and immobile.

I made several futile attempts to free the car from this trap, but it became evident that I would need a substantial truck to pull me out. Sitting there in despair, with the nearest house miles away, I pondered my predicament. As darkness began to creep in, I couldn't help but wonder: Would I have to spend the night in my car? How would I resolve this tomorrow? And where would I find something to drink? I was parched! My mind buzzed with a flurry of unresolved thoughts.

Lost in my distress, I stood by the roadside, contemplating my limited options, when suddenly, a bus rounded the corner, gradually slowing to a halt.

Without me asking, twenty men jumped off the bus and gathered around my trapped vehicle. With incredible strength and coordination, they pushed and heaved it out of the ditch. I watched in astonishment, deeply touched by their spontaneous kindness and compassion.

As soon as they were done, the men calmly returned to the bus, bidding me farewell with a wave before disappearing into the distance. The entire episode unfolded within a matter of minutes, leaving me in a whirlwind of emotions. I was overcome by this unexpected turn of events, which saved me from hours of anguish and uncertainty.

But what had just happened? The people on the bus had sensed my desperate need and responded without hesitation. They offered their assistance without any expectations of reward. This selfless act, driven purely by kindness, reinforced in me the notion that we should always be prepared to extend a helping hand to those in need. These opportunities to make a difference often arise naturally, requiring minimal time and effort on our part, yet provide genuine aid to those who require our support.

I have been on the receiving end of countless acts of kindness throughout my life. Inspired by gratitude towards those who have helped me, I consider it both an honour and a privilege to assist others. If we embrace the chance to contribute positively to the lives of others, we foster a cycle of kindness and compassion that uplifts us all.

Mean Girls and the Power of Forgiveness

While I was on my weekly paper route, there was one house I dreaded visiting: the home of identical twins, Ann and Susie. They were the epitome of 'mean girls', always sporting perfect hair and impeccable outfits.

One day, as I approached their house to collect the newspaper fee, their vicious dog seemed ready to pounce on me from behind the door. Instinctively, I raised my foot to defend myself. This act of self-preservation angered the twin who answered the door, as she accused me of being mean to her beloved pooch.

From that moment on, whenever one of the twins opened the door, I was met with snarky remarks in a condescending tone. 'Why are you always here? You're such a loser. Go bother someone else,' she would say, before shouting to her mother, 'The paperboy freak is here.'

To my surprise, whenever their mother arrived to pay me, she would apologize for her daughters' rudeness and show genuine kindness. It was clear that she saw beyond their behaviour and understood the importance of treating others with respect.

The twins' torment didn't end at their doorstep; they continued their name-calling at school, targeting not only me but others who didn't fit into the popular 'it-crowd'. For those of us not part of the inner circle, their attention was a dreadful thing, as it encouraged others to follow their lead.

Twenty years later, during a summer visit from Bangladesh to meet with my parents, I found myself at Walmart, standing in the checkout line behind the twins' mother. To my surprise, she greeted me warmly and inquired about my life. I shared that I worked in Asia for USAID.

In response, she mentioned that Ann was aspiring to pursue a similar career path. She asked if her daughter could reach out to me for some advice on breaking into the international public health field. Although reluctant due to my past experiences with the daughters, I felt a sense of obligation towards her and reluctantly agreed.

Two weeks later, I received an email from Ann. Her tone was upbeat and respectful as she inquired about my work and how I had entered the field. As I read her message, I realized that I still harboured some resentment towards the twins for their petty ways. Feeling compelled by a sense of responsibility, I responded with a brief reply. However, as I ended my response, I added a statement confronting her about her rude behaviour all those years ago. I couldn't help myself. I had to say something.

Weeks later, Ann's response arrived, filled with profuse apologies. She clarified that it was never her who had spoken meanly to me—it had always been her sister, Susie, who greeted me at the door. She expressed her embarrassment and remorse for Susie's behaviour, offering a sincere apology for what her sister had put me through. She also confessed that she had many regrets for her own actions during that period of her life. She realized that her behaviour was childish and hurtful to so many.

On that day, tears streamed down my face unexpectedly. I was taken aback by the emotional release triggered by her genuine words of remorse. This made me realize the incredible healing power of a heartfelt apology. It had the ability to liberate a person from long-held resentment. Inspired by this experience, I decided to let go of other similar hurts from my past and embrace forgiveness.

This encounter taught me that a genuine and sincere apology can work wonders. It has the power to mend old wounds and bring closure, enabling individuals to release pent-up grievances. It was a powerful reminder of the importance of forgiveness and the freedom it offers—to both the forgiver and the forgiven.

A Simple Act of Kindness

Years ago, charitable fundraising took place at the neighbourhood level. My mother, a staunch believer in each person's responsibility to support our world, would often receive requests from organizations like the American Heart Association and the American Cancer Association, seeking her assistance in raising funds.

Upon receiving a package containing a donation box and a letter authorizing her to collect money, my mother would go from door to door, reaching out to our neighbours and appealing for their generous contributions. Each time she went, she would raise up to $100, a substantial amount back then, and send it off to the respective organization.

As a child, I would do my best to be away from home whenever she received one of these packages. Why, you ask? Simply because she would often enlist my help. However, on one unfortunate afternoon, I wasn't quick enough to escape her clutches. She cornered me and earnestly implored, 'Can you do something for your old mother? Can you assist in collecting money for the American Cancer Association? It would mean the world to me. I need to pick up your sisters and go grocery shopping.'

Reluctantly, I asked, 'Do I really have to do this? Why am I always the one who has to do these things?'

'Because it is important,' she replied passionately. 'It helps people in need. With these funds, scientists can work towards finding a cure for cancer. Wouldn't that be an extraordinary accomplishment? Don't you want to be a part of this compassionate process?'

'No, I don't,' I retorted stubbornly. 'I just want to go out and play with my friends.'

With a gentle yet firm tone, she responded, 'I understand that you may not want to do this now, but someday you will look back and realize how significant your small role has been.'

Fast-forward to 2017 when I received the devastating diagnosis of prostate cancer. As I contemplated the necessity of a prostatectomy, I consulted several surgeons to ensure I made the best choice. Thankfully, the operation went smoothly, complications were minimal, and the prognosis appeared favourable.

During one of my follow-up appointments with Dr Wong, my surgeon, I recounted my childhood fundraising experiences. He smiled warmly, placing his hand on my arm, and spoke words that will stay with me forever: 'Over the years, remarkable individuals have dedicated themselves to research, striving to enhance cancer treatment. The favourable outcomes you are experiencing today are a result of years of experimentation, refining techniques and approaches. Without their tireless efforts, the aftermath of your surgery would have been vastly different, burdened by numerous side effects. What if one of the dollars you collected had contributed to this process. Have you ever thought about that?'

I realized then that the countless people who selflessly collected donations for good causes over the years had helped to make possible the medical procedures we rely on today. As the adage goes, 'every little bit helps'.

It was a humbling revelation that forever changed my perspective. Something that seemed completely irrelevant and meaningless in my life as a child, seemed to come back to me as a blessing. My mother was right, I did look back and realize that my small role in collecting those funds had significance.

A Difference in Perspective

During my time working for the development agency USAID, I had the incredible opportunity to live and work in Bangladesh for nearly five years. It became one of my favourite places.

On one of my vacations within the country, I decided to take my two sons on a trip to the city of Chittagong. However, the journey proved to be quite challenging as the road we travelled on was filled with an eclectic mix of cattle, rickshaws, and pedestrians, and it was a six-hour trip.

While I was accustomed to driving my Land Rover around my neighbourhood, venturing outside the city was considered too treacherous for a foreigner like me. Any mishap caused by an expatriate could potentially incite mob violence. To ensure our safety during our visit to Chittagong, I had my driver, Sushanta, take the wheel. He was an incredibly skilled driver who understood how to negotiate these complicated roads.

As we navigated a busy roundabout, a rickshaw driver halted suddenly in front of us and we ran into the back of his vehicle, damaging his left tyre. Although the accident was really nothing, within minutes, a sizable crowd enveloped our car.

'Please remain in the car,' Sushanta urged. 'Lock the doors. I will handle this situation.'

Feeling a surge of anxiety, I couldn't help but inquire, 'Will everything be alright?' The crowd was swelling rapidly, and my apprehension was mounting.

'He will demand money, especially from a foreigner like you,' Sushanta replied. 'His demands will likely be very high.'

'I'm willing to pay whatever is necessary. Just prevent this from escalating further,' I responded, my voice reflecting a mix of concern and determination.

Sushanta got out of the car and purposefully strode about 50 yards away, a tactic to divert the crowd's attention. Despite his efforts, numerous onlookers pressed their faces against the car windows, eager for a glimpse of the foreigners.

My two sons, aged four and six, began to feel increasingly uneasy. They bombarded me with questions, their innocent voices tinged with apprehension. 'Why are all these people staring at us? What's happening with Sushanta? When will we be able to leave?'

Despite my own fears, I reassured them with what I hoped was a calm and soothing tone. Through the car window, I could see Sushanta engaging in a heated exchange with the rickshaw owner, the commotion attracting more and more people.

After what seemed like an eternity, Sushanta finally returned and uttered, 'I am deeply sorry. I did everything within my power, but his demand was excessive.'

Eager to resolve the matter and commence our journey, I asked, envisioning an astronomical sum, 'How much?'

'Three hundred,' he responded solemnly.

I presumed he meant $300. Relief washed over me, grateful that the dispute was nearing its conclusion. Retrieving my wallet, I prepared to hand over the US currency.

'No, sir. It's 300 Taka. I apologize for the confusion,' Sushanta clarified, regret evident in his voice. 'I tried my best to negotiate, but it took considerable time to bring them down. I am truly sorry.'

'Only 300 Taka?' I exclaimed, taken aback. 'That's approximately $5.'

'Yes, sir. They initially demanded 500 Taka. It was quite a challenge to lower their expectations. Once again, I apologize for any disappointment.'

While my inclination was to offer a more generous sum, Sushanta advised against it, saying, 'Don't you dare do that. Accidents happen all the time and if we give more, it will drive up the fees. People will seek to have an accident to get this kind of money. It will result in people being hurt. Please trust my judgement, sir.'

I realized the importance of respecting Sushanta's advice and his understanding of cultural norms, so did as he suggested.

To my surprise, despite the seemingly paltry amount, the rickshaw driver accepted the cash with genuine delight, a broad smile illuminating his face. It was clear that he was happy.

For Sushanta, however, surrendering 300 Taka felt like a personal failure.

Why Focus on the Bad When There Is So Much Good?

Years ago, I used to engage in lengthy conversations with fellow passengers on airplanes. As I've grown older, however, I tend to do this less often. Instead, I close my eyes and try to rest.

On a recent trip from Vancouver to Ottawa, I found myself seated next to a middle-aged man named Bob, who had an inclination for conversation. Bob wasted no time in introducing himself and spent the next twenty minutes venting about his life's myriad problems. He bemoaned the need for a new roof on his house, his dissatisfaction with his job, the rising cost of living that hindered his vacation plans, and his frustration over not being able to purchase a coveted new car he had set his sights on months ago.

All of Bob's words focused on the obstacles he faced, punctuated by his frequent lamentation, 'I don't understand why I always have so many problems. Why me?'

When Bob finally concluded his litany of grievances, I couldn't help but say something in response. I posed a series of questions to him: 'Do you have a home? Can you work without worrying about losing your job? Is your family safe and in good health? Do you experience love and happiness in your life? Do you have some savings in the bank?'

To each question, Bob responded with a simple 'yes'.

Seizing the opportunity, I then took several minutes to illustrate how many people in the world live without access to clean water, sufficient food, stable employment, healthcare, education, and the freedoms we often take for granted.

Finally, I offered my perspective, saying, 'Considering your answers, it seems that your life is relatively good compared to countless others who are forced to endure dire circumstances. Have you considered counting your blessings and shifting your focus towards the many positive things you possess instead of fixating on what you lack?'

For a fleeting moment, Bob seemed to contemplate my words. But then, without missing a beat, he dived back into his problems and obstacles, seemingly impervious to any alternative viewpoint.

Personally, I adhere to a philosophy that helps me maintain a positive outlook. I like to tell myself that things will go well 50 per cent of the time, and that they will be challenging for the other 50 per cent. I see obstacles as an inevitable part of the human experience. That way, I don't sweat it when problems do arrive.

But I've observed that around 90 per cent of the time, things work out okay anyway—so I feel like I've done better than expected.

Over the years, I've found it's best to avoid fixating on the negative aspects of our lives and to concentrate on the positive instead.

If you want to navigate life's challenges, learn to appreciate the blessings that go unnoticed.

Not Everything Has to Be a Crisis

During a visit to one of the large home supply warehouses in the USA, I found myself wandering the aisles in search of a specific tool. Lost in thought, I stood there, glancing at the aisle descriptions, oblivious to the world around me.

Suddenly, a middle-aged woman approached me and asked politely, 'Excuse me, could you tell me where I can find floor tiles?'

Caught off guard, I didn't initially register her words. Sensing my distraction, she repeated her question with more urgency, 'Can you please help me find the floor tiles?'

Realizing that she was addressing me, I quickly turned to face her and responded courteously, 'I apologize, but I'm not sure where they are. If you check the signs above the aisles, I'm confident you'll be able to locate what you're looking for.'

Despite my intention to be helpful, the woman was visibly upset and walked briskly away. I couldn't understand why. Moments later, she returned with a store supervisor. Unbeknownst to me, they stood behind me while I was engrossed in examining a tool.

Unexpectedly, I heard a voice say, 'Why didn't you assist this woman in finding her tiles?' asked the supervisor. 'And where is your nametag?'

Startled, I turned around to discover the supervisor was addressing me, and before I could respond, the woman launched into a passionate tirade, expressing her frustration, 'What kind of store is this? I ask for help, and all I receive is a rude response. Is this how you treat customers? Do you want to lose valuable business?'

Confused by the sudden confrontation, I tried to explain, 'I'm sorry, but I don't work here. I'm just another customer.'

As I stood there bewildered, it dawned on me. I was wearing a bright orange polo shirt, strikingly like the one worn by the store's floor employees. Both the woman and the supervisor must have mistaken me for a negligent worker.

Responding sincerely, the store manager offered a heartfelt apology, while the woman stood there, unsure of what to say.

Without missing a beat, I took charge and invited them to follow me. They hesitantly obliged, and I led them along the main aisle until we found a sign that read 'floor tiles'.

Turning to the woman, I said with a smile, 'I believe this is what you're looking for. I hope you have a pleasant day.'

With that, I went back to looking for my tool.

When I tell others about this experience, people often suggest I should have expressed my anger and demanded a full apology, but I respectfully disagree. We all make mistakes, and this was a simple misunderstanding that didn't warrant escalating into a full-blown crisis.

By choosing to overlook their behaviour and granting them grace, I found that in this case at least, compassion and understanding were enough to defuse a tense situation.

I Helped Make Him Famous But Then I Couldn't Afford Him

In Nepal, a country well-known for its abundance of talented artists, I decided to commission an oil painting. After stumbling upon a remarkable local artist named Andy, I approached him with a photograph of the famous dust-bowl scene, seeking to bring it to life on canvas. Negotiations ensued, and despite my status as an intern on a tight budget, we managed to reach a fair and affordable price.

What was initially supposed to be a four-week project turned into a prolonged twelve-week endeavour. Each time I visited Andy's shop, I was disappointed to hear that the painting wasn't ready yet. Frustration began to creep in, clouding my excitement.

Eventually, the day arrived when Andy presented me with the completed painting, and my frustration turned into pure elation. The artwork was nothing short of breathtaking, a testament to Andy's undeniable talent and skill.

Buoyed by this extraordinary creation, I commissioned three more paintings from Andy, despite the recurring delays. Each time, my patience was tested, but the result never failed to amaze me. Andy's craftsmanship was consistently incredible.

As I eagerly awaited the completion of my fourth painting, I ventured to Andy's shop, only to find him absent. Seeking to leave him a message, I approached a neighbouring painter who happened to be acquainted with Andy. I asked him to relay my message, at which point the painter burst into laughter, leaving me bewildered.

After regaining his composure, he asked, 'Were you the one who commissioned four paintings from Andy?' Confirming his suspicion, I nodded, eager to understand the reason behind his amusement. To my surprise, he pulled out a nearly finished canvas of the fourth painting I had commissioned. It was then that he revealed himself as Sunil, the true artist behind the masterpieces. Andy had hired him to paint the artworks on his behalf, explaining the long waits. Sunil apologized, explaining that he only painted when inspiration struck him.

When we finally met, I confronted Andy, expressing my dissatisfaction with his deceptive arrangement. From that point on, I decided to work directly with Sunil, recognizing his remarkable talent and dedication to his craft.

As I delved deeper into Sunil's astonishing body of work, I noticed a recurring theme surrounding women's issues. Captivated by his thought-provoking creations, I suggested an exhibition to showcase his incredible paintings. Humbled and overwhelmed, Sunil said the idea exceeded his wildest expectations.

Motivated by my belief in Sunil's extraordinary talent, I took it upon myself to arrange the grand event. Through my connections, I managed to secure the attendance of the US Ambassador as the keynote speaker, along with representatives from UNICEF and UNDP.

The exhibition proved to be an astounding success, propelling Sunil from a painter catering to tourists to a recognized artist in the local scene. The press coverage lauded him as 'an up-and-coming painter with immense talent'.

Six months after the exhibition, I approached Sunil once again, this time with a new photograph in hand, seeking to commission another painting. As he assessed the image, he set a price that was nearly ten times higher than our previous projects. Perplexed, I asked him why.

Sunil smiled graciously and replied, 'You made me famous. Now, people recognize and value my work. I cannot express enough gratitude for your support. However, this new cost reflects the demand and recognition I have gained.'

Although his revised price exceeded my financial means, I left our meeting with mixed emotions, disappointed that I couldn't afford his services, yet content that he was receiving the compensation he rightfully deserved.

Sometimes, latent talents go unnoticed until they are brought to the surface. Once recognized, it is only right to remunerate individuals according to their exceptional abilities. While the change in Sunil's pricing did not favour me personally, it allowed him to earn a living that was more in line with his immense talent. Deep down, I found solace in knowing that I had played a small part in his journey towards recognition and success.

Treasured Memory

Growing up abroad, my two sons often heard tales of my childhood adventures in Connecticut, particularly stories surrounding the dazzling fireworks that illuminated our town every Independence Day. I vividly painted the scene for them—crowds gathering on Mill Pond field, laying down blankets, and eagerly awaiting the spectacle. Intriguingly, one tale stood out: I described how we would return to the site the following morning to look for coins that had slipped from the pockets of the mesmerized spectators.

During a summer visit to my parents, we decided to relive the tradition. As we sat on our blanket, my sons expressed a keen desire to wake up early and embark on a coin-hunting expedition the next morning.

At 7 a.m., they were already waiting for me, filled with anticipation. Together, we strolled to the field, ready to discover the remnants of last night's celebration.

Twenty minutes passed, and their enthusiasm began to wane as the coin count remained at zero. Sensing their frustration, I surreptitiously discovered five spare coins in my pocket. Inspiration struck—I decided to sprinkle a bit of magic into the moment. Tossing a quarter to the side, I declared, 'There's one.'

Damien triumphantly retrieved it, securing the first victory. Brandon, not to be outdone, grumbled, 'I was going to pick that up.'

Undeterred, I assured them more treasures awaited. I discreetly tossed a dime and a nickel to the left, pointing and asking, 'Do you see anything?' Brandon, eyes sharp, scooped up the hidden coins.

The game continued for an hour, the same coins disappearing and reappearing, each rediscovery met with unbridled joy. Returning to their grandmother's home, my sons regaled her with tales of their monumental finds. A knowing wink from me promised an explanation later.

That evening, I handed each of them two crisp dollar bills, declaring it the grand total of their treasure. As time passed, the memory faded into the recesses of my mind.

Years later, the topic resurfaced. To their friends, my sons recounted the tale of the field and the abundance of discovered money. Realizing the need to dispel the illusion and come clean, I sat them down and revealed the truth. Their faces reflected a mix of surprise and disappointment—another example of their father's playful deception after the tales of Santa Claus, the Tooth Fairy, and the Easter Bunny.

In the end, the magic of childhood gave way to the realities of growing up, leaving behind cherished memories of a whimsical treasure hunt on a summer morning.

Am I Living My Life All Wrong?

When I was sixteen, I discovered Tolstoy's poignant short story 'The Death of Ivan Ilych'. Ivan Ilych, a young man raised in Russia, followed the conventional path of privilege: attending the right school, marrying the right woman, securing the right job, and steadily climbing the social ladder. Like so many, as life progressed, he found himself drifting away from his initial idealistic aspirations.

It wasn't until a fateful accident left him with a chronic injury and ample time for reflection that Ivan Ilych confronted the harsh reality of his existence. In the face of imminent death, he agonizingly realized that his life had been grievously misspent, devoid of genuine purpose. Regrettably, he had arrived at this sombre revelation too late to correct any of his previous choices.

This story left an indelible mark on my own journey. Over the years, I have encountered many people like Ivan Ilych, who become suddenly aware of the dissatisfaction haunting their lives. Frequently labelled as a 'midlife crisis', this introspection stems from a variety of sources. Some lament their unfulfilled professional ambitions, unrealized personal growth, or untapped artistic and creative potential. Others believe they could have made a greater impact in healing the world. Many of us have either experienced such a crisis first-hand or witnessed it in someone we know.

When I turned forty, I too found myself caught in the clutches of this existential crisis. I confronted the painful realization that I had veered off course, forsaking my values and engaging in work that left me unfulfilled. At the time, I was working for USAID in Thailand. I had left a country-based programme in Bangladesh to take on a regional role for the agency. I was dividing my time between doing public health work and addressing the topic of human trafficking. While both were full-time jobs, I felt that I was getting mired in administration, without enough field work to be fully in the game.

Feeling like I needed to devote all my attention to human trafficking, I decided I needed a significant change. Eventually, summoning the courage to take a leap of faith, I left my comfortable job with the US government to embrace a new role at the United Nations, dedicating myself to combatting human trafficking within an entirely different realm. While it was a significant cut in pay and benefits, it was what I felt my heart and soul needed at that time in my career.

The reassuring truth is that it is never too late to change our lives. We need not resign ourselves to regret, accepting it as an inescapable fate.

To embark on this transformation, we must cast a penetrating light upon ourselves—one that reveals our present truth: our circumstances, values, actions, behaviours, aspirations, dreams, and even our shortcomings.

Ideally, when we reach the twilight of our lives, we should harbour few regrets and savour the meaning and purpose that have permeated our existence.

To reach that point, it is vital to regularly take stock by posing essential questions: 'Am I truly happy? Am I pursuing the life I desire? Am I aligning my actions with my deepest aspirations?' We must remember that the course of our lives remains within our grasp, even when it seems devoid of choices.

You Will Buy It Because You Can't Help Yourself

During the early days of my career, I had the extraordinary opportunity to travel to Pakistan on four separate occasions. Our purpose was to evaluate public health programmes funded by the US government. Accompanying me on these assignments were two highly experienced consultants, seasoned professionals with years of international expertise. As a young and insecure newcomer, I was fortunate to support them in any way I could.

While in Islamabad, our routine often included an intriguing excursion to a carpet shop that held a special place in the hearts of my colleagues. Situated within one of the city's upscale hotels, this establishment offered a captivating experience. Following our dinner, we would venture into the shop, immersing ourselves in its rich tapestry of colours and designs.

For those who have not experienced such a shop, let me paint a picture. As we entered, we would be greeted with a warm cup of tea, a gracious gesture of hospitality that set the tone for what was to come. Engaging in casual conversation, we would soon find ourselves surrounded by a symphony of carpets being tossed onto the floor; one after another. Over the course of an hour, a breathtaking selection of up to a hundred carpets would be meticulously presented for our consideration.

With each new addition to the display, the shop owner or one of his knowledgeable employees would regale us with a tale. They would describe the number of stitches in a particular carpet, its place of origin, the arduous months dedicated to its creation, and other fascinating details.

While I occasionally attempted to escape this mandatory ordeal, my experienced companions always insisted on my presence. The carpets, though seemingly small and exorbitantly priced to my untrained eye, held an allure for them that escaped my understanding.

As the hours drifted by, my colleagues would carefully select one or two carpets that spoke to them. Meanwhile, I remained seated, disinterested, and bored while feigning otherwise.

However, on one occasion, the shopkeeper, sensing my indifference, approached me directly. 'Do you not appreciate my carpets?' he inquired, his gaze fixed upon me.

'Sorry, they are simply not my cup of tea,' I responded politely.

A prolonged pause ensued before he spoke again. 'I will place a collection of carpets in front of you. I cannot predict which one it will be, but I assure you that you will discover something you adore. You will be willing to pay an amount that surpasses your wildest imagination for such an object. This will happen today.'

I regarded him sceptically, but curiosity got the better of me. 'You genuinely believe I will leave with a carpet?' I asked, my tone laced with disbelief.

'Yes,' he responded confidently, a glimmer in his eyes.

Smiling wryly, I agreed, 'Very well, show me what you have.'

As I sat there, feeling self-assured and prepared to prove him wrong, an unexpected turn of events unfolded. A carpet was casually tossed in my direction, and as my eyes beheld its magnificence, I was struck with awe. The design, the vibrant colours, the elaborate patterns—everything about it was breathtaking. It felt as if it were somehow intricately connected to my very essence.

'Do you find this one to your liking?' he asked, aware that he had captured my attention.

I hesitated for a moment, caught off guard by the undeniable attraction I felt.

'No,' I stammered, flustered. 'I'm not interested. But could you please tell me its price?'

He disclosed the figure, and it was staggering—a sum that exceeded all reasonable expectations. Without missing a beat, he continued, 'We don't choose carpets; carpets choose us. Each of us possesses a unique set of patterns and colours that resonate with our souls. When you see one of these carpets, there is no mistaking it. This is your carpet. Go ahead and try to walk away. You can't.'

He was right. I was hooked, I loved it. Ten minutes later, I paid the man and walked away with something I thought I'd never have. From that point forward, I understood.

This story illustrated the transformative power of unexpected experiences. It highlighted the unpredictable nature of life, where moments of surprise and shock can lead to actions or decisions that defy one's preconceived beliefs and expectations. It was a good learning experience for me, opening my mind to the myriad of possibilities that I often ignored as irrelevant to my life.

Honouring My Mother's Memory

I was embarking on a personal retreat to Lantau Island in Hong Kong for the first time in years, seeking solace and rejuvenation, when something strange happened on the ferry. An overwhelming sense of my mother's presence enveloped me.

As I sat in the open-air seating area, gazing at the turbulent waves, tears streamed down my face—a rare occurrence for me. The last conversation I'd had with my mother took place over seventeen years ago, while I aimlessly wandered through a department store in Bangkok. She was about to undergo a routine back operation and, in her hurried state, managed to utter, 'I can't talk now. Your father and I are heading out. The operation is tomorrow. Don't worry, I'll catch up with you afterwards. I love you.'

A day following the surgery, while walking along a corridor in the recovery area, she was struck by a massive heart attack caused by a blood clot. She was gone in an instant.

At the time, I was living and working in Thailand, and civil unrest had led to the closure of the airport. I was in shock, unable to return home to mourn my mother and console my grieving family. This compounded the trauma and unspeakable sorrow that consumed me. For months afterwards, upon waking up, my instinctual impulse was to reach for the phone and call my mom—only to be struck with the brutal reality that she was no longer here, forever beyond my reach.

Over the years that followed, I never truly allowed myself to mourn my mother deeply. She rarely crossed my mind. Even in my countless LinkedIn posts, where I shared childhood stories, I seldom mentioned her.

Sitting on the ferry that day, a profound realization washed over me—I had refrained from writing about her because her passing remained an open wound, too raw and painful to confront. Closure had eluded me, and this wound had yet to heal. Perhaps it never will, for grief is said to be the price we pay for love.

Upon reflection, I recognized that my mother was undoubtedly the most influential person in my life. Her vibrant spirit radiated exuberance and laughter, illuminating every room she entered. She embodied charisma, compassion, wisdom, and love. Yet, I also recall moments of sadness and withdrawal in her. A frustrated housewife in the suburbs, she possessed the potential to thrive as a CEO, but circumstances confined her to the role of a supermom raising six children.

During moments of crisis throughout my life, she was my pillar of support. With open arms and words of solace, she had a remarkable ability to lift my spirits. It was she who instilled in me the passion to dedicate my life to helping others. Through her actions, she modelled the importance of public service and caring for those in need.

Realizing that I had not fully processed her passing, I devoted an entire day to reflect on the cherished memories and the lasting legacy my mother left behind. With tears flowing freely, I sensed that my shattered heart was gradually healing. Thus, I felt compelled to write these words, a tribute to her life and the indelible impact she had on mine.

Mom, I love you and miss you dearly.

9

Lessons from the Workplace

Work plays a significant role in many aspects of our adult lives. It occupies much of our time, contributes to our financial stability, and, when we find it enjoyable and fulfilling, can infuse our days with a sense of purpose.

But it does more than all that. It intertwines with our self-image, shaping how we perceive ourselves and how others perceive us. It has the power to impact our overall well-being, influence our physical health, emotional state, and mental resilience.

When we are successful in our endeavours, it is exhilarating. It serves as a testament to our hard work, dedication, and commitment. The joy that accompanies such accomplishments validates our efforts and boosts our self-esteem. It reinforces our belief in our abilities and propels us to further achievements. These moments of triumph are like beacons, reminding us of the fulfilment that can be derived from our work.

Yet, it is during the darker times of failure that we encounter opportunities for growth. When our plans go awry, we are faced with the harsh reality that success is not guaranteed. This is when we gain a deeper understanding of ourselves. In moments of failure, we are forced to confront our shortcomings. We have the chance to analyse and dissect what went wrong, then identify areas for improvement. It is through this self-reflection that we can develop new strategies, refine our skills, and hone our abilities.

An Ethical Dilemma that Cost 10,000 Children Their Lives

During my tenure doing public health work in Nepal, I often found myself faced with challenging decisions. One instance stands out: our acute respiratory infection response programme led to a fall in the annual number of child deaths by 10,000. We can be sure this drop was a direct result of our work because the country was annually registering 30,000 child deaths a year before the programme. Post-programme, that dropped to 20,000.

It was a great triumph for us, and it did not go unnoticed. Soon after, another donor expressed interest in adopting our programme. While, naturally, we would have liked to keep running the programme ourselves, we had limited funding at the time so had to carefully consider this donor's offer.

Although the prospective donor was a major multinational development agency, in the past they had taken over our programmes only to discontinue them after a few years.

Given the crucial role of this programme in saving lives, I had major reservations about their commitment.

Initially, I adamantly resisted the idea. However, under mounting pressure from the government, we reluctantly agreed. The decision weighed heavily on me from the very beginning, as I knew it carried significant life and death implications.

As expected, two years after the agreement, the donor reneged on their commitment, resulting in child mortality figures escalating back to 30,000 deaths annually. The situation unfolded exactly as we had feared, and it deeply troubled me.

Eventually, another donor stepped in to salvage the programme, but the process took a painstaking eighteen months to finalize. Tragically, during this long period of uncertainty and transition, thousands of children needlessly lost their lives.

These events continue to haunt me, and I still grapple with feelings of guilt. It is a constant reminder to me of the imperative to prioritize human life when confronted with similar choices.

Decisions in the realm of public health and other development sectors carry immense weight, with moral and ethical implications that cannot be ignored. We must always remain mindful of the lives at stake and strive to make choices that safeguard and enhance the well-being of those we serve.

Flash Flood

During my eight-year tenure in Nepal, much of my time was spent immersed in the field. Expeditions in our trusty Toyota Land Cruiser involved going around the country on visits to healthcare centres and hospitals. The trips were always meticulously planned.

But Nepal's challenging terrain posed a constant obstacle; to cover a mere 100 kilometres often meant an arduous five-hour journey. And the perils were not confined to rough roads alone. Depending on the season, there were landslides, daredevil bus and truck drivers, and cows with a seeming death wish to navigate, not to mention a host of other hazards.

On one of our ventures, our mission was to reach a remote hospital nestled in the Terai, the lower region of Nepal.

Though the skies above us were clear, ominous clouds loomed on the horizon and 10 kilometres beyond the main highway, we confronted a riverbed, stretching nearly 50 metres before us.

However, as the water was only six inches deep, we could cross it without incident and within half an hour we arrived at the hospital.

Our visit unfurled as planned. I met the hospital's administrator and staff, toured the facility, and finally, inaugurated the new surgical unit we had proudly funded. All this took less than an hour.

Just as we were preparing to bid our farewells, my trusty driver, Prakash, approached me with an urgent matter. He told me rain had fallen in the hills, and given the risk of a flash flood, we should cross the river without delay.

As we reached the riverbed, the water had already swelled. It was now a foot deep and rising relentlessly. Prakash looked at me with an earnest concern. 'I'm not sure about this crossing, sir. It could be very dangerous. The water is steadily rising.'

I asked him, 'What if we opt not to cross? Are there any accommodations nearby?'

He replied, 'No, there are no hotels or guesthouses on this side of the river. Should we take the risk?'

'Let's proceed,' I resolved.

Crossing the river proved far more treacherous than we had envisioned. Midway through, we turned our gaze upstream and were met with a horrifying sight—a towering surge of water, nearly three feet deeper, accompanied by an assortment of debris.

As this torrential deluge engulfed our vehicle, its sheer force threatened to overturn it. We found ourselves teetering on the brink of disaster.

In those harrowing moments, minutes stretched into what felt like eternity. The spectre of imminent peril loomed large, and our very survival seemed uncertain. I genuinely believed our journey might end in tragedy.

Yet the expertise of my seasoned driver, Prakash, emerged as our lifeline. With incredible skill, he steered us to the safety of the opposite shore.

Upon reaching solid ground, the two of us stepped out of the vehicle and hugged each other in an embrace that remains etched in my memory.

Reflecting on that heart-stopping experience, I can't help but recognize the recklessness of my decision to forge ahead. I had unwittingly placed both of us in grave danger. It's an incident that continues to haunt my nightmares, yet it serves as a powerful reminder of the need to prioritize safety above all else. The inconvenience of waiting, in hindsight, might have been a minor annoyance, but it would have ensured our safety.

In the end, this harrowing incident left an undeniable mark on my consciousness. The lesson it taught me: never compromise safety for expediency, no matter the circumstances.

Walk the Talk

During one of my many visits to Cambodia, I encountered an incident that shed light on the inconsistency between the conduct of certain human rights experts and the principles they espouse. It happened during breakfast at a hotel, where I had arrived early to catch up on some work. I was there to attend a three-day conference related to human trafficking and human rights.

Moments after I arrived, a prominent human rights expert from Europe entered the breakfast area. After settling down at one of the tables, he approached the section where eggs were prepared, only to find the cook engaged in a phone conversation, causing a slight delay.

Rather than exercising patience, the human rights expert immediately launched into a tirade, berating the cook for making him wait. His verbal assault persisted for several minutes until the hotel manager finally came and intervened, inquiring about the commotion. The manager reprimanded the cook publicly, thoroughly embarrassing him.

I couldn't help but feel sorry for the cook, caught in such an unpleasant situation. While it was true that the cook had caused a brief delay, the magnitude of the human rights expert's response appeared disproportionate. In fact, the circumstances hardly warranted any reaction at all. To me, it seemed like a tempest in a teapot.

As I prepared to leave the restaurant, I approached the cook and expressed my regret over the incident, acknowledging that it shouldn't have escalated to such a degree. To my surprise, the cook burst into tears, sharing with me the reason behind his behaviour. He explained that his wife was undergoing surgery that day, and he desperately wanted to be by her side. However, with no one available to cover his shift, he felt trapped. The call he had received earlier was from one of the nurses at the hospital, adding to his emotional distress.

Had the human rights 'expert' displayed a bit of patience and granted the cook the benefit of the doubt, he might have discovered the depth of the man's personal struggles and offered empathy and compassion instead of condemnation.

This incident was a reminder that people working in the service industry carry burdens that may be hidden from view; the same burdens we all face. We should extend grace and patience to them whenever possible.

Many people face trials and tribulations in their personal lives, and a little understanding can go a long way. Likewise, it is imperative that we hold ourselves to the same standards we expect from others when we champion human rights.

This human rights expert made grand efforts on the global stage, but he failed to exhibit the same principles in his personal conduct. In my view, if you lack patience, empathy, compassion, and principled behaviour, then the human rights sector is not for you.

If you are doing this work, you should embody the values you promote. Walk the talk.

I Thought Our Plane Would Crash

In 1989, I found myself in Pakistan assessing a US government health programme, accompanied by the esteemed former US diplomat Ambassador John Blane. After concluding our afternoon's work, our itinerary involved a brief fifteen-minute flight from Islamabad to Peshawar. The aircraft, a small plane with two propellers and seating for eight, was virtually empty, with only Ambassador Blane and me as passengers.

While I had previously driven the 187-kilometre road connecting these cities, it was a treacherous journey to undertake at night due to reckless bus drivers, poorly maintained roads, and an array of horse carts, pedestrians, and roaming goat herds. For this reason, this flight was considered a safer alternative.

Moments before our departure, a furious storm descended, unleashing high winds, torrential rain, and flashes of lightning. Though I presumed we would wait out the inclement weather, the captain stated calmly, 'Hold on. It's going to be rough.'

Even before the plane cleared the runway, it began to experience violent turbulence, tossing us about as if we were a paper airplane caught in a gale. While Ambassador Blane appeared unfazed, I was overcome with fear.

The severe turbulence caused abrupt shifts in altitude and airspeed, at times rendering the aircraft almost uncontrollable. Within minutes, we found ourselves descending instead of ascending.

In a determined voice, the captain announced, 'It's too windy. I'm going to land. We'll wait and attempt again.'

After the pilot executed a formidable landing, we waited on the airstrip for a tense twenty minutes. The experience left me so traumatized that I seriously thought about disembarking from the plane altogether.

'Let's give it another try,' said the captain. And so, for the second time, we took off, endured a brief period of erratic flight, and touched down once again on the same airstrip.

Seeking reassurance, I turned to Ambassador Blane and pleaded, 'We should abandon this trip. It's really not safe.'

With an air of confidence, he snapped back, 'Sit down and stop complaining. These pilots are highly experienced. They know what they're doing, and they don't want to die. They'll get us there. Don't be such a baby.'

Though his words carried a certain harshness, they were precisely what I needed to hear to restore my faith in our safe arrival.

Finally, on our third attempt, the plane took off, jostling about for a brief period before ascending above the stormy weather, and ultimately landing safely. As we disembarked, the captain greeted us with a smile, remarking, 'I hope the turbulence didn't rattle you too much. This time of year brings plenty of storms. Enjoy your visit.'

Years later, I found myself aboard a flight from Bangkok to Hanoi accompanied by one of my interns from the United Nations. Thirty minutes into the journey, we encountered a prolonged spell of turbulent skies, lasting nearly an hour. I sat there, calm and composed, as the young intern's fear became apparent in his eyes.

'Will we be alright?' he finally inquired with great trepidation. 'Is there a risk of the plane crashing?'

Recalling my encounter with Ambassador Blane during our perilous flight decades prior, I responded to the intern with reassurance, saying, 'These pilots are experienced professionals who know precisely how to handle these situations. We will reach our destination safely. Don't worry, everything will be fine.'

In that moment, I saw the transformation I had undergone. It was a humbling realization. I had become the embodiment of my myriad experiences, resembling Ambassador Blane as I offered advice and reassurance to the next generation.

This journey had come full circle. It showed me the importance of drawing wisdom from our past encounters to guide and comfort those who come after us.

Our Management Style Is an Extension of Who We Are

During my time working in public health in Nepal, I had the privilege of collaborating with a remarkable doctor named Ganesh. He was a dedicated clinician working in a prominent public hospital, and over time, we developed a strong friendship. Whenever I visited Ganesh, we would sit down together and share a cup of tea, engaging in stimulating conversations enriched by his intelligence, articulation, and gentle disposition. I always enjoyed our discussions and valued his insights.

One day, Ganesh called me with great excitement, sharing the news that he had been offered the opportunity to lead a large department in a prominent hospital. I wholeheartedly congratulated him, genuinely thrilled for his well-deserved promotion. I had no doubt in my mind that he would make an exceptional boss, given his outstanding qualities.

Three months later, Ganesh called me again, his voice tinged with anxiety. He expressed his distress, revealing, 'They all hate me. They don't listen to me. I can sense the whispers and negative talk behind my back. I don't know what to do. I'm a terrible manager. I should never have taken on this role.'

Surprised by his plight, I responded, 'Ganesh, how can this be? You are one of the most likable individuals I know. People genuinely adore you.'

In a defeated tone, he replied, 'I followed the instructions of the hospital board. They insisted that I instil fear in my staff. They claimed it was the only way to lead effectively, to be strong.'

In that moment, I recognized the crux of his problem. The approach he had adopted was completely inconsistent with his authentic personality and deeply held values. I urged Ganesh to embrace his own leadership style, to be true to himself.

'But this is how hospitals are managed here,' he lamented.

In response, I suggested that he approach his role authentically, to be honest with his staff, and to establish a foundation of open communication and partnership with them. I encouraged him to discard the fear-based management style imposed upon him and instead lead with integrity and empathy.

A month later, Ganesh called me once again, but this time, his tone was more relaxed. He recounted how he had mustered the courage to apologize to his team for his previous harsh management style, acknowledging the offense he had caused. He humbly requested a second chance, and, to his relief, they granted it.

For Ganesh, the pivotal moment came when he decided to hit the reset button and align his actions with his true self. As he embraced this change, things improved immediately.

'I treated them the way I wanted to be treated,' he confided. 'That brought about the change.'

This experience reinforced a timeless lesson—as managers, it is imperative that we break down the barriers that hinder trust and impede open and honest communication with our staff. Each of us must embark on a leadership journey that is consistent with our unique personality, temperament, and approach, guided by authenticity and respect.

His Eyes Were Opened

During my tenure in Bangladesh, I often found myself guiding visiting guests through the vibrant local markets to give them a genuine glimpse into the country's rich culture. Being an avid photographer,

I had explored numerous captivating locations within the city, each with its own unique charm.

One day, a call beckoned me to accompany a gentleman named Harold to one of these bustling open markets.

In the course of our drive, I discovered that Harold was a highly successful businessman who had amassed his wealth through the sale of medical devices. This trip marked his first venture beyond the borders of the USA, and he candidly admitted to feeling a bit overwhelmed by the experience.

As we strolled through the market, I shared my insights into the local culture and offered the lessons I had gained from living three years in the country. As we continued on our way, Harold's demeanour shifted from cheerful to visibly stressed and overwhelmed.

On our way back to the car, Harold gestured towards a nearby slum area and inquired, 'What is that place?' Seizing the opportunity, I suggested, 'Let's go and see.'

For the next hour, we navigated through the labyrinthine alleys of the shanty town. Our conspicuous presence drew many curious inhabitants, who, true to the hospitable nature I had come to love, greeted us with kindness and enthusiasm.

During our walk, he witnessed tiny shacks that housed entire families, open sewers, excessive crowding, and other signs of dire poverty. The extreme sights, sounds, and smells were overwhelming for a new visitor.

Following this eye-opening excursion, I took Harold to the American Club, where our conversation delved into the myriad challenges faced by people across Asia and the world. We discussed poverty, education, health, and more. His expressions betrayed a deep shock at the revelations.

'I had no idea about these problems,' he admitted repeatedly.

'What you've witnessed here transcends geographical boundaries; it exists worldwide, including in the USA,' I responded. 'Issues persist everywhere. The key is to open our eyes.'

What transpired next caught me off guard. Harold looked at me and confessed, 'I feel so ashamed. It struck me as I walked through that place—I'm a selfish man. I have so much, yet I haven't done anything for others.'

In response, I offered him a warm smile, which seemed to surprise him. 'Why are you looking at me that way?' he asked.

'I am genuinely happy. During this visit, you opened your heart and mind to the realities of this world. Not only did you witness the challenges, but you also felt them. This is a commendable realization. Don't harbour shame for what you haven't done; rejoice in what you can or will do in the future. Many people observe but never truly feel.'

Occasionally, I witness such transformations—pivotal moments in a person's life when they are truly awakened.

An Unexpected Surprise

During my time working for USAID in Nepal, much of my time—about 40 per cent—was dedicated to fieldwork. These ventures involved traversing remote areas to visit health programmes, clinics, and health centres. While these journeys were often arduous and time-consuming, they presented us with invaluable opportunities to witness development initiatives in action and identify areas for improvement.

One particularly memorable expedition took place in the district of Solukhumbu, home to Mount Everest. As part of this trip, my team meticulously planned a 16-kilometre hike, encompassing visits to three health centres along the way.

We left on our adventure after an early morning rise, relishing a hearty breakfast. Arriving at the first two sites without incident, we engaged with clinic managers, interviewed staff members, and closely observed the services being provided. The impressive dedication and commitment we witnessed left a lasting impression on all of us.

As we proceeded towards our third destination, we unintentionally veered off course, finding ourselves utterly lost. By 2 p.m., the grim reality set in—we were hours away from our base in Phaplu and any semblance of civilization. The absence of local restaurants along the way compounded our predicament. We were famished.

With no clear solution in sight, one of my programme officers approached a random village house, seeking assistance. He humbly requested if the woman living there would be willing to prepare a meal for us, offering compensation for her time and efforts. Without a moment's hesitation, she graciously accepted the offer.

For nearly an hour, we were captivated by this elderly woman as she skilfully manoeuvred through the kitchen—cutting, chopping, boiling, stirring, and seasoning with an unrivalled finesse. It was a spellbinding performance. Not a single motion was wasted, every action imbued with purpose. She was an artist, crafting a masterpiece.

When the meal was served, the sight of the rice, dal, vegetable curry, chutney, and yogurt appeared very simple and modest in their presentation. However, as I took my first bite, I was utterly astounded. The flavours exploded on my palate, each mouthful an extraordinary sensation. I struggled to recall a meal that had ever been more appetizing. It was an experience that transcended the boundaries of taste, surpassing even the offerings of esteemed Michelin-starred restaurants.

When recounting this tale, I occasionally encounter sceptics who argue, 'Come on, Matt, you were in a picturesque farmhouse, overlooking majestic mountains, in the company of people you cherished, pursuing work you were passionate about, after a strenuous hike. Of course, the food tasted exceptional.'

While there may be some truth to their observation, I can indeed attest that few meals have left such a mark on my memory. On that extraordinary day, I came to realize that astonishing experiences can arise from the most unexpected places. Secondly, the pursuit of amazing food does not require opulent settings or extravagant resources, it can be found in the humblest of locations. Finally, I learned the significance of savouring the journey as much as the destination. There are rewards to be discovered within the spaces between, just waiting to be appreciated.

Every Time I Sent Him a Proposal, He Shot It Down

When I took on a new job in Bangladesh working for a renowned development agency, I was entrusted with the task of designing and developing several major components of public health portfolios. After carefully reviewing existing programmes and coming up with a list of potential improvements, I began submitting my ideas to my boss, Jay, through concise emails that outlined my thought process.

In response, Jay always countered with lengthy, detailed emails that shot down each and every one of my proposals. While this initially frustrated me, I couldn't deny that his writing was exceptional, captivating me with its clarity and insight.

At first, I questioned whether I had ended up in the wrong position, as it seemed I had acquired a challenging boss. Eventually, I mustered the courage to approach Jay and express my frustration. I said candidly, 'I don't understand why you never accept any of my proposals. I've presented you with at least ten ideas, and each time they are dismissed.'

Jay's response was a gentle smile accompanied by the words I had been longing to hear, 'I've been waiting for you to reach out to me. I don't know why it took you so long.'

Perplexed, I continued, 'So, what is it about my work that you find unsatisfactory? Why don't you accept any of it?'

With patience, Jay replied, 'It's because you're being lazy. You offer suggestions without providing any substantial backing. If you send me a thoughtful, detailed, and compelling proposal, I'll respond positively. Convince me with logical and practical arguments, and I'll let you know. The few sentences you've been sending are never enough, which is why I've been shooting them down.'

Could it truly be that simple? I wondered. 'Are you saying that if I can build a strong case for my ideas, you will accept them?' I asked.

'Yes, that's all it takes,' Jay said. 'If your proposal is supported by data, presents a clear analysis of the current situation, identifies what is working or not working, outlines necessary changes, provides an implementation plan, assigns responsibilities, estimates costs, and more, then I'll agree. If it lacks any of these components, I'll push back. You have to work for my approval.'

Heeding his advice, I began crafting comprehensive ten-page proposals that meticulously addressed every aspect—data, status, challenges, solutions, strategies, budgets, and more.

When I submitted my first detailed proposal to Jay, the response arrived within an hour—a simple, one-word email that read, 'Proceed'. I was now in business.

While not every proposal was immediately accepted, Jay would always afford me the opportunity to persuade him. If I could substantiate my assumptions with evidence and information, I would receive the green light. Otherwise, I revisited my approach and tried again. I came to relish these exchanges.

In retrospect, I also came to appreciate how much Jay had aided my professional growth. He taught me the importance of intentionality in my work, encouraging me to articulate my ideas with supporting evidence and thorough analysis. As my career progressed, I reaped the benefits of this approach on countless occasions.

Jay unexpectedly became one of my favourite bosses. As a manager myself, I strive to instil the same level of rigour and thoughtfulness in my team. I hope they, too, recognize and value the significance of this approach.

You Must Pay $20,000 for the Mistake You Made

Years ago, I found myself entrusted with the management of a health development portfolio for a donor agency. Acting as the intermediary between my agency and the funding recipients, I quickly became acquainted with the myriad rules and regulations that governed our operations.

During my tenure, one of the organizations I worked with made a routine request for a 'no-cost extension'. If granted, this would allow them to utilize the funds beyond the original contract end date. The process, involving a few forms to be signed, typically sailed through with 100 per cent approval within a week.

Just three days prior to finalizing the paperwork, I received a call from the organization, asking if they could proceed with a $20,000 conference. Reasoning that we were merely navigating through the labyrinth of paperwork, I gave them the green light to proceed. Though I was aware that bending the rules in this manner was not allowed, I assumed it was a harmless decision.

However, I felt less sure when our agency's financial officer paid an unexpected visit to my office and asked me, sternly, 'Did you authorize that organization to proceed with their conference?'

Sheepishly, I admitted, 'Yes.'

'Were you aware that this broke our rules?' she asked, in a grave tone.

Attempting to justify my actions, I replied, 'I didn't think it would be a big issue. We all agreed it was acceptable since we were simply waiting for the paperwork to be signed.'

She did not seem impressed. 'You do realize that you will bear the financial responsibility for the $20,000 they spent? Tell me how and when you intend to repay this amount.'

Suddenly, the gravity of this unexpected situation dawned on me. I had no inkling as to how I would come up with that much money.

For three restless nights, I couldn't sleep as I fretted over my mounting debt. Every possible solution and scenario raced through my mind, tormenting me.

Eventually, unable to endure the mental anguish any longer, I mustered the courage to visit the financial officer. I proposed a repayment plan that involved instalments spread over the course of a year—an arrangement that would enable me to meet my obligations, albeit with considerable strain.

She observed me intently for what felt like an eternity before finally responding, 'Have you learned your lesson from this experience?'

I nodded, acknowledging the gravity of my actions.

She continued, her tone slightly softened, 'You don't have to make any payments. My objective was to teach you a lesson—a reminder that rules cannot be broken. If you do, there can be dire outcomes. I can see you now understand this fact. I will sort this out this time around.'

That day, I learned the power of punctuating teachable moments with severe consequences. While I was greatly relieved to be spared the financial burden, the experience left a lasting impression on me and has guided me throughout my career ever since.

I realized that adherence to rules and regulations is not just a matter of formality but a cornerstone of integrity and accountability. That day, I resolved always to remain within the boundaries while navigating the complex world of admin. I know now that to do otherwise can have the severest of consequences.

The Power of Encouragement

Years ago, I found myself in need of a project administrator. Despite advertising the position multiple times, I struggled to find the ideal candidate, one who possessed the right blend of skills and qualities. However, a serendipitous encounter at a public health conference introduced me to a young man who would prove to be the perfect fit.

Throughout the event, this young man provided invaluable assistance to the participants, exuding efficiency, helpfulness, and a wealth of insightful ideas. His cheerful disposition and accommodating nature made a lasting impression on me, leaving me eager to learn more about him.

Yet, during lunch, I observed a rather perplexing scene—an interaction between him and his boss that brimmed with disapproval and reprimands. I couldn't understand what he could have done to warrant such a negative response.

Intrigued by this observation, I approached his boss later in the day and started a conversation. I told her that I was impressed with her assistant. I listed several actions he performed that really helped me that day. To my surprise, she dismissed my positive impressions with an eye roll, describing him as a frequent source of errors and trouble. She confessed that she regularly scolded him to 'keep him in line'. This revelation puzzled me even further.

Before leaving the conference, I handed the young man an application form for the project administrator position, asking if he knew of anyone suitable. He shook his head, prompting me to suggest that he consider applying himself. He took my advice, submitted an application, and ultimately, I offered him the job.

When he first started, he was very nervous and made a variety of mistakes. In response, I always answered with reassurance and encouragement, emphasizing that his missteps were insignificant, and that improvement would come with time. Gradually, as his self-assurance grew, the qualities I had witnessed during the conference began to shine through. The once-nervous young man transformed into an exceptional employee.

Years later, he approached me with a question, 'Why did you choose to hire me?'

I considered my response carefully. 'Because I recognized your untapped potential. You were intelligent, organized, and brimming with brilliant ideas. When I observed you at that conference, it was evident that your supervisor failed to appreciate your true value. She didn't grasp what you needed to thrive.'

Curious, he inquired further, 'And what was it that I needed to thrive?'

'The space to take risks, to try new things, and to fail,' I replied. 'For someone like you, your drug is "my faith in you". While you made some mistakes when you started, I did not make a big deal about them. In time, your nervousness went away. Now you have gone from being nervous and fearful to confident and capable. This comes from having someone believe in you.'

'How did you know this approach would work with me?' he asked.

'Because I once stood in your shoes,' I confessed. 'I had a similar experience early in my career. I was fortunate to have a supervisor who took me under her wing, enabling me to reach my full potential. She believed in me, and this allowed me to thrive.'

I firmly believe that a person who feels valued and appreciated will consistently go above and beyond expectations. Confidence flourishes in an environment of encouragement and support.

From Order to Anarchy

It was early July, the sweltering heat of summer in South Asia. I was making a routine visit to a remote government-sponsored health camp, a sprawling compound where two dozen tents were offering services to at least 2,000 people—all of them waiting patiently in line.

In regions where placing doctors permanently was unfeasible, these periodic health camps served as lifelines, offering essential medical services to people who had long been deprived of care.

My gracious host was a dedicated doctor overseeing the entire campaign. As we made our way through the compound, we stopped to chat with the waiting patients, all of whom wore contented expressions.

In that fleeting moment, I felt deeply impressed by what appeared to be a seamless operation unfolding before my eyes. It seemed to be meticulously organized, with effective systems and procedures to cater to the diverse needs of the many patients.

Just moments before I climbed into my Land Cruiser to go to my next site, a sudden public announcement pierced the air: 'The services provided by this health camp will conclude in one hour. Only those in line who reach the doctor within this timeframe will receive assistance.'

I watched as a wave of confusion washed over the waiting crowd. The announcement meant many people, some of whom had waited for days, would not receive the medical attention they so desperately needed.

In an instant, the fabric of order began to fray. Small groups of people began to huddle together, their frustration and anger palpable. Within minutes, the atmosphere turned tumultuous, the voices rising ever louder.

The tension in the air reached a breaking point, and then it happened—a burst of collective rage. What had been a serene scene just minutes ago transformed into chaos. People surged in all directions. The medical facilities were ransacked, the staff attacked, vehicles overturned, and medical supplies pilfered and carried away.

Never before had I borne witness to such a spectacle. Mere moments earlier, these very same individuals had appeared as model citizens; now, within the frenzy of the crowd, the boundaries between right and wrong had vanished entirely. It was a free-for-all, a maelstrom of chaos and lawlessness.

That day etched into my memory the precariousness of our society. The line between civilization and pandemonium proved exceedingly thin, easily breached by the slightest provocation.

Since then, I have observed two similar riots unfold, each culminating in the same catastrophic chaos. It seems that when caught up in an unruly crowd, individuals can lose their sense of self, reason, and rationality.

As human beings, we must confront the sobering truth that the possibility of such behaviour is within us all and take every measure to ensure it does not come to pass.

Social order, as I learned, can be astonishingly fragile.

The Talent Was Right There in My Office, But I Failed to See It

During my time working in Nepal, I supervised a multimillion-dollar public health programme. Two years after taking on this role, my office faced a big challenge in data collection and analysis. For months, we struggled to effectively manage the vast amount of data required to do the job. Recognizing the urgency of the situation, I raised the issue during a staff meeting and proposed seeking support from a consulting company, despite the uncertainty of securing the necessary budget.

Immediately after this meeting, my senior technical adviser approached me and asked, 'Have you spoken to Aaron about this?'

Puzzled, I responded, 'Why would I consult Aaron?' After all, he served as our secretary.

'Talk to him, and you'll understand,' my adviser insisted.

Intrigued, I approached Aaron, who was typically engrossed in his computer tasks. Despite having worked together for three years, I knew little about him. He remained quiet, rarely offering his thoughts.

'Aaron, I heard you might have insights regarding the data issue I discussed in the meeting,' I began. 'Do you have any suggested solutions?'

He appeared bewildered, his eyes reflecting uncertainty. I struggled to comprehend his reaction.

'After you brought up the topic months ago, I began experimenting with an idea,' he finally responded, hesitantly.

'Could you show it to me?' I inquired.

'It's nothing,' he said dismissively. 'I'm just a secretary.'

'Let me be the judge of that,' I replied with a warm smile.

Over the next thirty minutes, Aaron unveiled a data collection and analysis system he had developed in Excel. With each passing moment, I grew increasingly amazed by the sophistication, practicality, and efficiency of his brilliant creation. I was truly wowed.

'Aaron, what you've created here is the solution we've been desperately seeking. It addresses all our needs. Why didn't you bring this to my attention earlier?'

'I'm not a technical person, I'm just a secretary. I didn't think you'd be interested in anything I developed. We have technical experts for this kind of work,' he explained, with a hint of surprise in his voice.

'Aaron, all I can say is wow,' I responded, feeling a little embarrassed for not recognizing his latent talent and brilliance earlier. 'Your work will save us thousands of dollars. Based on what I've seen, we can implement this solution in other offices within our agency. Your contribution is truly remarkable.'

He was lost for words. I wondered if this was the first time he had been acknowledged for such a valuable contribution.

Over the following four months, we operationalized Aaron's tool, trained our staff on it, and began to use it in other offices. As time went on, we expanded Aaron's role, providing him with opportunities for growth and development. He surpassed his own expectations and embarked on a journey far beyond what he had ever envisioned.

This taught me the importance of seeking out the hidden talents of our team members, recognizing that they may extend beyond the boundaries of their designated roles.

Organizations that can tap into the unique skills and perspectives of their workers are likely to find they do not need external support. As often as not, the answer lies within.

Unintended Consequences

When I was a young professional, I had the incredible opportunity to visit nine countries alongside the former US Ambassador John Blane, who had served throughout Africa during his illustrious career. On one of our trips to Rwanda, he shared with me a story that has remained with me ever since.

The tale revolved around a desert country that harboured a stable population of 150,000 cattle for many years. Curiously, this number remained unchanged despite the outbreak of a contagious disease every year, which claimed a sizable portion of the cattle. Essentially, the disease acted as a natural regulator, ensuring the equilibrium of the animal population.

Recognizing the treatability of this disease, a funding agency approached the government with a proposition: they could inoculate all the animals, effectively eradicating the ailment and allowing the cattle herds to flourish. It seemed like an ideal solution, resolving a persistent issue.

The programme was swiftly implemented, and as expected, the cattle population began to thrive. The numbers surged from 150,000 to 300,000, then 500,000, and even reached a staggering 650,000. On the surface, it seemed an unmitigated triumph.

However, a critical factor had been overlooked. The grasslands available to sustain these burgeoning herds proved woefully insufficient. The voracious appetite of the cattle led to the rapid depletion of the grass and its roots. Consequently, the barren land, devoid of vegetation, succumbed to the merciless winds that carried away vast amounts of precious topsoil.

Before long, the dire consequences of this oversight were manifest. The available food supply became woefully inadequate, unable to meet the needs of the swollen cattle population. Many of the once-flourishing animals succumbed to starvation and their numbers plummeted. What was once a thriving herd of 650,000 was reduced to fewer than 70,000.

This cautionary tale is a reminder that in the world of development, there are no quick fixes. Only the most meticulous research and in-depth analysis will do, and both of those require time and patience. Rush it and you will be plagued, like those poor cows, by unintended consequences.

Overcoming One of My Worst Days Ever

On one of those challenging days during my time in Thailand, life seemed determined to throw every possible obstacle my way. The morning started with me oversleeping, setting the tone for what would become a series of unfortunate events.

Attempting to flag down a taxi proved futile, leaving me stranded in a sudden downpour without an umbrella. By the time I reached the office, I was soaked and promptly summoned by my boss, only to be unjustly reprimanded for something beyond my control. Frustration mounted as she refused to listen to my side of the story.

During lunch at the cafeteria, an unexpected crunch revealed a bone in my fried rice, chipping my tooth. Returning to my desk, I received an email from a donor, delivering a devastating blow by withdrawing funding for our ongoing programme. The day took another hit when one of my best staff members informed me of her departure from the project.

As if that weren't enough, an email from my son announced a change of plans, preventing our anticipated weekend together.

The cumulative weight of these disappointments reached its peak at 5 p.m. when, desperately seeking an escape, I spent an additional thirty minutes attempting to find a taxi. The final straw came when, opening the taxi door, I collided with a passing bike rider, injuring my hand in the process. Fortunately, the bicyclist walked away unscathed.

Retreating to my apartment, I slumped onto the couch, emotionally drained, defeated, and engulfed in a sense of despair. In that moment of vulnerability, I reached for a tall beer in the refrigerator when a sudden pause overcame me.

Without fully understanding why, I began to reflect on the broader context of my life. Despite the day's relentless challenges, I realized I had a job, a loving family, a roof over my head, financial stability, good health, supportive friends, and a promising future. It dawned on me that many of the human trafficking victims I worked with faced a daily struggle without these basic comforts.

A wave of guilt washed over me as I recognized the insignificance of my momentary hardships compared to the profound challenges others endured. Yes, we all experience bad days and encounter obstacles, but it's crucial to maintain perspective. Counting our blessings and acknowledging the positives in our lives can provide a powerful antidote to negativity and remind us of the many reasons we have to be grateful.

* * *

Our work holds a profound influence on our lives. It shapes our sense of purpose, provides us with financial security, and impacts our overall well-being. While success brings joy and validates our efforts, it is in times of failure and disappointment that we can find the greatest lessons. These experiences offer us the chance to look inwards, learn from our mistakes, and emerge stronger, more resilient, and more determined in our pursuit of success.

Confronting my own imperfections has been a deeply personal journey, one requiring vulnerability and a willingness to acknowledge my own fallibility. But looking back on my failures, I see how many sowed the seeds of personal growth. From the ashes of disappointment, resilience has taken root, enabling me to rise stronger, more empathetic, and more understanding than before.

Part Three

Epilogue

How Do the Pieces Come Together

Looking back at the stories in this book has helped me to understand the incredible journey that took me from my humble beginnings to becoming a global force against modern slavery.

In a sense, this was a journey that had two beginnings. One came in adulthood, when an encounter in Nepal took me face to face with the harsh reality of forced prostitution, shaking me to the core. This was a clear turning point, a moment in time that ignited my passion and propelled me on a mission to combat human trafficking that would take me through more than forty countries over the following thirty-five years.

But there was another beginning to my journey, the genesis of which is harder to pinpoint. This one is not about any single moment in time, though it stretches back to my childhood. I see it when I look at my experiences as a mosaic and the seemingly disparate pieces come together to form a coherent, beautiful whole.

This is why I have split this book into two distinct parts. Part one was about the many victims, perpetrators, and tireless activists I have encountered. Their first-hand accounts were meant to confront the reader with the profound suffering in our world, much as I was confronted with it during that encounter in Nepal. I hope these stories may provide the same spark in others that ignited my own passions all those years ago.

Part two focused on my personal journey. The idea was to show that my trajectory from a reserved New England boy to a global anti-trafficking activist was not predestined; that it was a path open to any one of us.

My early experiences may not have directly shaped my later career, but they influenced my values, passions, and sense of purpose. From the threads of these seemingly ordinary events, the tapestry of my character was woven.

As a shy and introspective boy, I quietly observed the world's injustices and became sensitive to the struggles of others. Meanwhile, the close-knit nature of my small-town upbringing instilled in me a sense of community and collective responsibility.

In adolescence, personal failures and inadequacies cultivated empathy, while navigating peer pressure, forming friendships, and becoming aware of societal issues taught me how to use my voice for change. Puberty taught me resilience and how to overcome obstacles—qualities that proved invaluable later in life.

In adulthood, work not only brought financial stability but also influenced my self-image and overall well-being. Success brought joy and validation, while failure provided opportunities for growth. Confronting imperfections led to resilience, empathy, and understanding.

In essence, my life's journey reflects the power of seemingly ordinary experiences to do something extraordinary—to shape values and purpose and, ultimately, to be a force for change.

Change the World

Curating and plumbing the depths and emotions of my memories has been a powerful exercise. I have recalled people, places, and experiences that I had long buried and sifted through them to discern the lessons learned.

I also explored the question 'How does one find one's calling and destiny?' For most of my life I've felt there was an invisible hand guiding me, beyond my control, in everything I've done. For example, I didn't intend to become a public speaker—I was terrified of it—yet today I speak to corporate, college, and faith-based groups nearly every week.

That's true of writing books as well. I never considered myself a good writer, but I had the discipline and the follow-through to write several novels during the same years as I was grappling with the suffering of modern-day slaves. At the same time, my daily posts on LinkedIn forced me to remember the people and the forces that have shaped me since my childhood. Looking back at my life and assessing has been exhilarating, painful, and sentimental all at once.

Over the years, I have come to believe that each and every one of us can spread kindness and make a difference—we just need to listen to the voice of the everyday hero within us. Collectively, we have the capacity to heal more people, feed more people, educate more people, resolve international and community issues, and help others when a disaster or conflict arises.

There is a potential hero in all of us. It is a voice of good, of righteousness, of action, and of love. In this modern world of ours, this voice often receives too little nurturing. Too often, our inner hero lies dormant and our potential for doing good is never fully realized.

But when stirred, this noble side of ourselves can wake us up to current issues and problems and encourage us to help.

Heroism is that part of our mind that whispers into our thoughts, urging us forward, to step up, to act, to get involved, and to do the right thing. There are times when this voice is silent and times when it screams. We can try to ignore it, but that way lies regret and despair.

This inner voice helps us see the path ahead, often persisting until we listen and respond. It's the voice of goodness; it motivates us to help. To be involved. To have a sense of purpose.

Over the years, as I've found myself faced with choosing the comfortable path or sacrificing my time and energy to help others, I've learned to surrender. For me, a hero is someone who makes the effort to learn about something and, in his or her own way, does something to help.

You don't have to completely change your lifestyle to tackle a problem. Big change starts with acts as simple as educating others, sending money to a struggling charity, or volunteering at a local non-profit organization for a few hours a week. Heroism is all about acts of goodness, big or small. They all add up.

Here are nine simple actions you can take to be part of the solution:

1. Educate Yourself

- Learn about the different forms of human trafficking, its root causes, and its prevalence globally and in your community. Stay informed about current issues and trends.

2. Raise Awareness

- Use your voice to educate others. Share information on social media, organize awareness campaigns, and tell friends and family about the signs and consequences of human trafficking.

3. **Support Anti-Trafficking Organizations**
   - Contribute to, or volunteer with, organizations that actively work to combat human trafficking. These organizations often provide victim support and work towards changing government policies.

4. **Be Vigilant**
   - Be aware of your surroundings and report any suspicious activities to law enforcement. Trafficking victims are often hidden in plain sight; your vigilance can make a difference.

5. **Campaign**
   - Support legislation aimed at preventing human trafficking, protecting victims, and prosecuting perpetrators. Write to your elected officials and join campaigns for stronger anti-trafficking laws.

6. **Support Fair Trade**
   - Choose products and services that are certified as fair trade. Supporting ethical businesses reduces the demand for products and services linked to human trafficking.

7. **Know the Signs**
   - Learn to recognize the signs of trafficking, such as individuals who appear fearful, submissive, or controlled, or situations where people are not free to come and go as they please.

8. **Volunteer**
   - Offer your time and skills to local organizations that work with at-risk populations or support victims of trafficking. Volunteering can range from mentoring survivors to assisting with awareness campaigns.

9. Encourage Ethical Practices
- Encourage businesses, especially in industries prone to exploitation, to adopt ethical practices in their supply chains. Consumers can influence corporate behaviour by supporting companies committed to fair labour practices.

Meanwhile, if you take just a few core messages from this book, I would like them to be these:

- Collective actions have the greatest chance of impact. An army of ordinary people working together can make extraordinary change.
- For change to happen, we need to unite lots of different types of people—all sharing their unique experiences and skills together.
- Collaboration is essential because we are stronger when we work together as a community rather than passing the buck to a handful of paid professionals.
- We should all feel inspired to act because the issues of our time are urgent—and they affect us all in one way, shape, or form. As the poet John Donne once wrote, 'No man is an island.'

I leave you with the words of anthropologist Margaret Mead: 'Never doubt that a small group of thoughtful, committed citizens can change the world; indeed, it's the only thing that ever has.'

www.ingramcontent.com/pod-product-compliance
Lightning Source LLC
Chambersburg PA
CBHW020538030426
42337CB00013B/897